Shelley Prowse
2002

Dear Sarah
Best birthday wishes
July 2005.

FOOL'S PARADISE

Fond memories
always. XX

Steve Braunias

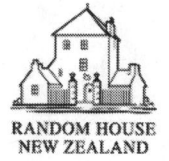

RANDOM HOUSE
NEW ZEALAND

Thanks to C.K. Stead for his permission to reproduce part of 'Tohunga Crescent' on p. 13; and to Bob Orr for his permission to reproduce part of 'Creosote' on p. 181.

A RANDOM HOUSE BOOK
published by
Random House New Zealand
18 Poland Road, Glenfield, Auckland, New Zealand
www.randomhouse.co.nz

First published 2001

ISBN 1 86941 483 7

Design: Jenny Nicholls
Layout: Kate Greenaway
Back cover photograph: Ken Downie
Cover photograph: Janek Croydon
Cover image work: Alistair Lang
Cover design: Jenny Nicholls

Printed by Griffin Press

CONTENTS

INTRODUCTION

THIS GUY WALKS INTO A COLUMN and starts blathering about himself. Each week in the *Listener* magazine, my 'Fool's Paradise' column fits quite snugly on page 94, right at the back, as far away from the action as possible, to lead a quiet, preoccupied existence. I like it there. I mind my own business. I make the subjects up as I go along, but the truth is that I have always intended the columns as a kind of report on New Zealand.

The tearooms in two-story towns, the passing seasons. The mangroves, the hot pools, the abundance of trouts. That sort of thing, set only within these shores, and on the shores, wherever there's a drink to be had and a village idiot to celebrate and a quiet corner to read a book about such New Zealand experiences as whaling or mining. They are postcards, memos, notes, pages from a diary, sketches, memoirs, brief items of possible interest; in short, the following selection, which first appeared in the *Listener* over two centuries (1999–2001), are a manner of journalism. Reviewers are welcome to agree.

In any case, this was the idea when I began writing the columns in February 1999. A brief glimpse into the kind of monomania that guides a columnist can be had from my clandestine meeting with the *Listener*'s new editor, Finlay Macdonald, when we met at a discreet downtown bar one night to discuss why I should leave *Metro* magazine to join him at the helm of New Zealand's leading current affairs title. He banged on about the virtues of the magazine and his ideas of editorial content. 'Yes, that's grand', I said. He fixed me with a burning eye and told me of the crucial role I would play.

'I'll drink to that', I said. And then he muttered something about how it might be of possible interest to readers if I wrote a monthly column, just like I did in *Metro*. 'But the *Listener* comes out every week,' I pointed out, 'so the thing to do would be to write a weekly column.'

Eventually, after the poor devil knocked back his full glass and saw his vision of New Zealand's leading current affairs title go blurry at the edges, he raised his head and said, 'That's a lot of work'. I told him I would find the time. And so every column has been written at home, on a Monday evening after work, to the tune of cups of tea and coffee – milk, no sugar – and generous donations to the tobacco industry, which needs all the help it can get.

So can the columns. My thanks, then, to Finlay and to the Listener's band of sub-editors and designers for their invaluable assistance; to those readers who have been kind enough to write in encouraging my delusion that 'Fool's Paradise' is a fit pastime for my Monday night vigil; to Random House, for what you are about to receive; and most of all to Jenny Nicholls, for her cover design of the glamorous lamington, and for loving a fool.

CAPITAL OF NEW ZEALAND

JOHN CLARKE, the comedian previously known as Fred Dagg, told me something interesting about the letter Z when I talked to him in Melbourne last year. It was primarily interesting because – really, I know no shame – I had often thought much the same thing myself. He said all New Zealanders abroad look out for a capital Z whenever we read a newspaper or a magazine; that we have an instinct for it, almost literally a homing device, on the off chance it might spell New Zealand.

Maybe he was drawing attention to his own habit. I failed to ask. My concentration dawdled off at that point in our interview. I was too busy thinking you don't have to leave the country to keep your eyes peeled for the big Z. I do this at home all the time, with a book, and suspect it's a shared, common experience, a kind of collective unconscious specific to these two islands.

Reading is like a dream. The mind is elsewhere, wherever the book takes you. But you wake up whenever the Z zig-zags its way into view; your eyes instantly widen, you feel like the author is tapping you on the shoulder. Your name is being called out. A capital Z – it can only mean one thing. New Zealand.

Unless it's a book about Greek legends, in which case you might reasonably expect to see a lot of Zeus. And yet New Zealand turns up in some unlikely pages. Last weekend, I bought *Sir Vidia's Shadow* by Paul Theroux. It's a mad and often shrill memoir of his friendship with the writer V.S. Naipaul. With friends like Theroux, you don't need stalkers; the book reveals (and reveals, and reveals, and reveals) Naipaul's pomposity, monomania, treachery, refusal to pay for meals, and various other failings over the past 30 years.

But there's a hilarious account of a luncheon in England, sometime around 1974, hosted by Naipaul and his wife Pat. Theroux bowls along, in the company of Lady Antonia Fraser and her husband, the Conservative MP Hugh Fraser, a fop called Julian Jebb, and a young couple called Malcolm and Robin. Malcolm and Robin are from New Zealand.

New Zealand! Great! A similar jolt hit me a few years ago when I read Chekhov's obscure 1884 novel *The Shooting Party* – obscure, because he wrote it under a pseudonym, and also because it isn't very good. It includes a scene where Count Alexaney Karneev hears about a case of wife-beating. He explodes, 'This is barbarous! This is like New Zealand!'

Top line, and about the only thing I remember from that slight book. From reading *Sir Vidia's Shadow*, it seems we're still savages; worse, we're in the flesh, and getting right up Theroux's delicate snoot. He is at that time the popular author of *The Great Railway Bazaar*. Malcolm's first words to him are, 'Beaut book, Paul!' Robin says, 'It gets dark so early here. And listen to that wind.' The appalling accent whistles in Theroux's ears: 'If I had not heard New Zealand in her nasalised *dahk* I would surely have heard it in her *weend*.'

Later, Malcolm bores everyone by reciting poetry, and arguing. Theroux: 'A beaky Kiwi in the throes of pedantry, Malcolm stuck his pink face into Antonia's pale one . . . Speaking in his New Zealand accent he could not make much of a point; he sounded as if he were satirising himself.'

The luncheon is a disaster. Mocked, patronised, and finally avoided, the wretched New Zealanders ruin what might have been a lively gathering. No one has a good time, although Theroux briefly entertains himself as he imagines whisking Lady Antonia off to a tropical island to have really good sex. He concludes his account of that dreary day by telling us what happened to his fellow guests. Lady Antonia left her husband for Harold Pinter. Hugh Fraser died of a broken heart. Pat Naipaul was diagnosed with cancer, and died. Julian Jebb commited suicide. Damningly, witheringly, he adds: 'No news of the New Zealanders.'

Poor devils! Where are they now? Are they still married, have they remained bungling and gauche? What do they make of Theroux's cruel, brilliant memory of their existence? Perhaps they returned home and said to their friends, dahkly, 'We met Paul Theroux in England. Not at all what we imagined . . . '

I like to think they got over it. But the fact is I enjoyed that chapter tremendously. Laughed my beaky Kiwi head off. As a New Zealander, I love reading about our foreignness, our otherness – drawn in by that capital Z, those three straight strokes, as familiar as family; at the end of the world, the final island, we are held by the last, most far-fetched letter of the alphabet.

6 March 1999

MANGROVIA

TOO RIGHT I read it here first. 'Four out of every ten New Zealanders are in advanced stages of work burnout,' claimed last week's cover story in the *Listener*. Great. Credulous to the point that I once went along for the ride when a friend claimed toy stores sold a doll called Mr Gullible (squeeze it, and it peeps: 'I believe you!'), the news of widespread job stress soon had me convinced I was among that miserable percentage.

It hit me last Tuesday. I had a hard day in the office. There seemed so many things to do and such little time in which to perform them badly. The phone rang its head off. Someone kept piling lots of press releases on my desk. I spilled mince on my shirt. In the backstage of my mind, I fretted about income tax and cholesterol levels. It's true that it pleased me greatly when a squadron of administrators measured up my office to install a red velvet couch. But this happiness hoofed its fleet-footed way out as soon as they left, and the phone rang, and the mince stain darkened, and the press releases babbled their way towards the ceiling.

All I needed was a headache. I got a headache. I ransacked the first-aid kit. A few useful ampules of sodium nitrate, but no disprin. Apparently the policy here is to lock such narcotics away in a secret tin, probably kept in the basement, in case someone gets a big-time thirst for that good, good taste.

Four out of every ten New Zealanders: I'm with you. I'm there. Burned to a grimacing crisp – it builds up, you know; I've been in this job for, oh, five weeks – I did an Elvis. I left the building. Hang the job. Tear up the contract.

It was lunchtime. I considered going to a cafe to buy an organic pork sandwich, but doubted its authenticity. I've never met an organic pig in my life. Instead, I mooched off to a nearby bay. That was all right. And then I turned to stroll alongside a walkway beside a creek.

It's not supposed to be a very nice creek. They say it's a bloody disgrace. They are wrong. True, it's dreadfully polluted, and choked by stormwater, and it stinks and looks black as the worst night of your life, and has nowhere to go but straight to hell.

Yes. But things are different at high tide. There is life. After a minute's mooch down the walkway, I saw an eel. A long, dark, shimmering eel, just beneath the water's surface, its tail drawing the letter S as it swam below my shadow. 'Hello!' I blurted out loud, and this top bloke kept me company for about 10 minutes, as we headed upstream at the same casual pace.

I loved that eel. He had fins like ears, and a small, thin gob; he stopped for a while to chase a breadcrumb, but could only bunt it with his head. Poor devil! 'Animals,' wrote Whitman, 'do not sweat and whine about their condition.' This eel had every right. The breadcrumb was not for eating.

We parted on good terms, and I walked on, stopping here and there to throw mangrove pods into the creek – they take root in the mud, sprouting up in a ring of things called pneumatophores, thin as sticks, spitting out salt and breathing life into the mangrove plant. Mangroves adore creeks, the silence, the slow tides, the darkness. Obscurity and mystery: the mangroves browsing the banks of the creek, the water green and mesmerising.

Further on I leaned over a bridge, and watched a heron filling its face. A heron has four mustard-yellow toes, like bones, and lifts its thin legs daintily above the mud. Dipping its exaggerated beak into the water, it clearly didn't give a toss about income tax or

11

cholesterol levels.

Crabs ran for their lives. A shoal of fish passed by. An eel – possibly my old mate – wriggled about. A couple of herons roosted in the tops of trees. I stood and looked at these fellows long and long. Hang the job, etc. I was placid, and cured, in this remote, ancient corner of the world, just around the corner from the not particularly harmful demands of work.

Nature, eh? So calming, so Other. There's nothing new in that, and I'm grateful. Total, utter irrelevance – more, please.

20 February 1999

THE TRUTH ABOUT MANGROVIA

Tohunga Crescent
 you could say begins in the
mangroves and goes on up to the
stars
– C.K. Stead

THE TRUTH about mangrovia – the word I made up which refers to the four columns in this book devoted to the mangrove swamp creek which runs behind my flat – is my truth about Auckland. This in its dreams city, an isthmus rattling with cellphones, a cowtown with one horse and a fancy saddle, thinking itself better than anywhere else, where I moved to in 1990 because it did in fact offer something no other city in New Zealand could. I got work here. A city with a salary, a city of arrivals: for years and years, this has been the one big smoke in town, the destination of the urban drift. All visitors ashore. And you make it your home, or you continually feel as though you are passing through – Auckland is always at rush-hour. I continually feel as though I am passing through. Just visiting, thanks for the money.

But this is going too far, this is too pat to be entirely believed. The weather's good and the bars are open late, and if you want something to eat there is ham on the bone at the Avondale racetrack. The grand houses of Remuera have the importance of bank vaults. The wind in the cabbage trees sounds like the snipping of scissors. It's great to be alive and look upon the harbour so blue that it seems double-coated. Bob Orr walks down the street and sees it flowing like the Ganges, he sees elephants and miracles, and if Auckland is good enough for New Zealand's finest living poet, then it's really good.

And the very best thing about Auckland, the thing that holds it together, pastes it onto the page, sucks it dry and then fills its boots, spits out the salt and breathes in through its mouth, drowses grey-green in the sun and barely notices the wind, tickles the fish and is a red-light district for the birds, is on the fringe of everything and the heart of it all, is mangroves.

For a long time I didn't even know the word for those flat, useless swamps. No one ever talked about them, no one so much as mentioned their existence. I used to stare at the creeks and the parched mudflats at low tide and the vast mangrove hedges with loathing – they were all over the shop, ugly and sickly and unsuitable for bathing, good for nothing. It wasn't until I picked up a book at a library remainder bin for 50 cents that mangroves were properly revealed.

Auckland at Full Stretch: Issues of the Seventies, published by the Auckland City Council and something called the Board of Urban Studies at Auckland University, contains a worthy and thoroughly boring series of essays about town planning, transport systems, housing, feminism, health needs, civic government, etc. But there is one terrific piece of writing by Professor Keith Sinclair, 'Experiences of Auckland and Her People', where he simply and sincerely gets to the point of the city. 'The only logic in this talk is the logic of the landscape and seasons,' he writes. 'That is the first thing about Auckland. Life here is lavish. Nature is kind.' And: 'Our land is all edges, all shores, on a gulf, two large harbours and endless creeks.' Also: 'Auckland is the gulf and the harbour and the mangroves and the mudflats.'

Soon after reading Sinclair's essay, I wrote my first story about mangroves, for *Metro* magazine. I discovered Auckland, came to love the hidden jungle of its heart, while I was writing that story and mucking around in the mud on various discreet shores. All that wetness trickling and oozing to and from all those shores – mangroves are a subtropical sweat in this city of tides.

I've been rewriting that *Metro* story for four years. Mangroves are now the first thing that comes into my head when I'm out of town and think of Auckland, the first sign of home when I fly into the airport and take a cab through the suburbs. The green sheets of water at high tide, the stark brown moon-surface mud at low tide. The mangroves in a bunch. The wading birds.

And so I spend a lot of time fishing out rubbish that Auckland wankers throw into the mangrove creek that runs behind my flat, and I suppose you could say my efforts display a civic pride. It sort of is like that. I just want it to look clean, to look as good as it should in the eyes of the herons and the mullets and the eels, because they are my fellow Aucklanders.

My eight-page blather in *Metro* subsequently won a Qantas Media Award for best environmental feature. The prize was a slow-growing red pine rimu in a pot. Good one. I like it very much. What I really wanted, though, was a slow-growing mangrove swamp, complete with mud and crabs and shags and rubbish – I wanted my own patch of wet, steaming Auckland.

MILK, NO SUGAR

BLUFF OYSTERS arrived this week. I want me some. Raw, on ice, with lemon, and pepper, maybe even an insouciant hint of soya sauce. Or perhaps fried, the fat mindless flesh tarted up in a dress of batter. A carpetbag steak stuffed with Bluff oysters is another option; my God, that would pull the rug right out from under your tongue; and because we are all allowed to dream of riches, of luxuries, of soft, gasping nights of love, it would most definitely be rather bloody nice to scoff down a crayfish served alongside the quivering visitors from the deep south.

All this is by way of trying to pass myself off as a man of sophisticated tastes. I know about good food. I like it. But I also very much like and adore an honest scoff. Few pleasures in everyday life beat an egg sandwich and a hot cup of coffee poured straight from the pot at a friendly New Zealand cafeteria. None of that muck known as espresso, as focaccia, as tofu, as cappuccino, as feta, as pesto; I've said it before and I'll say it again, the only good food that ends in an unusual vowel is the bright, slippery cheerio.

As such, I thought I knew exactly what I was doing a few days ago when I bowled into the Dominion Road shops in Mt Eden for a haircut. I like knowing exactly what I'm doing. It makes a change from work. I had trodden this path many times before: I could add it up like simple arithmetic: a $10 haircut at Karl's, followed by an egg sandwich and a hot cup of coffee poured straight from the pot at Cafe 99. Brilliant. Freshly shorn, reinvented as a fellow of temperate hair length, and then fed and watered while I sat at a table covered with a gingham cloth, I would step back into public life, tidy, whole, immaculate.

First things first. I waited patiently in the barbershop as Karl scalped some old bloke, and read a copy of *Picture Post* and the letters page of *New Zealand Fisherman*, and tapped my cigarette into the ashtray; the morning was warm, the sky a mess of skittering clouds; work could hold. I knew exactly what I was doing.

Eventually, I stepped up to the big chair and submitted to Karl's art. It took about 10, 15 minutes. Once again, the maestro came through. I looked all right. Now lighter on my feet, I walked around the corner to Cafe 99 for the other sum of these parts, for the kind of honest scoff that restores my love of this country.

It wasn't there. In its place was a mural painted on a board right up against Cafe 99's front windows. The mural, I had to admit, was cheerful: it showed a blue sea, palm trees, yachts: it put you in mind of the Caribbean, of wide open holidays beneath a sun that never went out. But I was standing in darkness. Cafe 99 had closed down. The mural was a falsehood erected by a demolition company. Inside, through the open door, two workmen whistled merry tunes as they picked their way over the remains of the floor.

'No,' I whimpered. Hoping against hope, I ambled up and down the street – perhaps I had the wrong address. I looked longingly into shop windows. There were vacancies in the security industry advertised at Work and Income Support. Geoff's Emporium promised 'Talk Of The Town Prices' and 'Geoff's. It's Wild!' At the TAB, Sirius Deluxe was favourite to win the 310m Wobbley's Bar Dash at the Forbury Park greyhound track. Total Health bragged of 'The Cactus Drink That May Help Cure Millions!' I thought it improper to enter Florence Beamish Ladieswear, SW to XXXOS, and blandly read the message on a sandwich board outside the Sri Chimnoy Vegetarian Cafe: 'Peace begins when we realise that the world does not need our guidance.'

I returned to stand outside what was once Cafe 99. The sign above the awning was still in place: 'Teas. Coffee. Lunches.' Next door were Hunt and Gaunt Optometrists. How entirely and appallingly appropriate. I felt hunted, I looked gaunt, I couldn't believe what I was seeing.

But of course I had seen it all before. Cafe 99 was a small, good thing, simple and necessary, just like other tearooms which have closed down in the last, grasping decade. The market is for espresso and similar slop, not egg sandwiches and a hot cup of coffee poured straight from the pot.

Well, I'm sick of it. I would love to hear about the real New Zealand coffee lounges which are still in happy existence. Please, send in their names, their details. Speak of their glad treats. I'll compile the list. Write to 'Teas. Coffee. Lunches' at the *Listener* address. We'll celebrate these establishments. Join the campaign to help save them. New Zealand needs your guidance. I need a cup of coffee.

24 April 1999

Rococo. 63 Ohoho St, basement level. Hours: Lunch, Monday-Tuesday 12pm-12.45pm. Dinner, Sunday, 6pm-6.30pm.

ADMISSION TO a certain kind of bar and restaurant these days is a privilege, not a right, and this excellent thinking is taken to its logical conclusion at Aleister Crowley's delightful new venture, Rococo. Our party of four were met at the door by trained bank staff who accessed our financial records before we were allowed through the door. Grooming specialists in Rococo's discreet salon were then called to pass judgment on our appearance. Fair enough. I for one thought their stinging rebuke of Hubert's goatee – at his age! – was long overdue.

Such preliminaries certainly whetted one's appetite. Seconds after we were seated at an Italian vinyl banquette, we were served, gratis, an eggcup of free-range chicken gizzards flavoured with walnut. Victor thought his was slightly overdone, but Hubert relished its piquancy, and Mavis remarked that last Tuesday she paid a Korean philosophy graduate $45 to have sex. It was at this juncture that our waitperson arrived to seek permission to ask whether we might be ready to order our entrées.

We were all taken by this charming apparition. 'Nice buns,' said Mavis, while Hubert and Victor praised his high cheekbones, his watery eyes, and his marvellous blend of servility and cravenness. 'Open wide,' I asked him. I gave him a satisfied nod: I do like a waitperson who flosses.

Hubert started with the asparagus, roasted beet and bocconcini terrine flavoured with walnut ($89.50), while Victor went for the grainfed smoked oysters ($125.50). Was I in the mood for surf, or for turf? In the end, I sat on the fence, and decided on the truffled hummus with pickled onions and fiddlehead ferns ($176). Mavis has always been a surf girl, and ordered two bottles of Sacred Hill Riflemans Hawkes Bay 97 ($58 each).

For the three of us who were eating, it was difficult to pass comment, because it took only eight seconds to finish our portions, which were served in the middle of 86cm bowls. But during her second bottle, Mavis passed wind, which was still warm by the time it reached us, and epitomised what she is about: saucy flavours with an integrity not displayed often enough.

There is a vibrancy to Rococo's atmosphere, although minus the pose quotient. That could be because no one else was dining while we were there. On the music front, George Michael's lovely version of 'Roxanne' soothed even Mavis, while Victor and Hubert came back from the gents' extolling the range of handcreams.

For mains, I voted for the chilled lasagnaettes of fresh dolphin ($1,400), while Hubert tried to assert his masculinity by choosing the spice-rubbed grilled goat's head flavoured with walnut ($2,545). Victor elected to have the shiitake served with baked craap beneath a piece of piis ($3,600). Mavis asked the waitperson to serve her Krug Vintage ($590) by the teaspoon. 'Gold star status!' I cried out. 'Ample!' roared Hubert. 'A vigorous piis!' yelled Victor. It was fun to raise our voices, and necessary, too, because our 480cm bowls demanded so much space that we had to sit at separate tables.

By dessert, Mavis was unbuttoning her blouse and wanting to have a dip in the fishtank. I left Victor to sort her out, and retired to the ladies to powder my nose. I do like cocaine after a meal, and appreciated Rococo's range of Italian glass straws as I hoovered up a gram. When I returned to the table, Victor was telling Hubert how he had donated $20 over the phone to victims of an earthquake, I think it was, in Mozambique. 'That's lovely,' I said, but reminded the men that it wasn't proper to discuss politics over dinner.

I admit to being a trifle disappointed by my trifle ($290). It wasn't up to head chef Jean-Claud Van Bulow's usual standard, when he worked at Sodom. But Victor announced he was mightily pleased with the muscat Beaumes de Venise custard served with Milk Arrowroots ($380), and Hubert lapped up his shavings of Egyptian orange pips on crushed ice flavoured with walnut ($7,090). Mavis drank from a hot waterbottle filled with a 1994 Church Road Chardonnay ($45), and slapped the waitperson's face. He was a good sport about it, so we tipped him $5.

'Mrs Trout!' shrieked Crowley, as we prepared to leave. 'You look divine! How did you like my little bistro?' I told him what I shall now tell you: 'Reasonably priced. In the aesthetics department, perfect in its triangular presentation. The obvious philosophy you have embraced here is stripped-down and unpretentious. As for the Italian toilet paper, it was adult and assured, with a textural eminence and an intoxicating flavour.'

He clapped, and so should you – it was one of my best speeches. To conclude, I heartily recommend Rococo, but also suggest that you invite a doctor, preferably an emergency resident. Sadly, our night out was Mavis's last supper. Poor girl. Only 43, and such a loss to her chosen field of public relations.

15 April 2000

FREE LUNCH

USING THE kind of influence that can open any door in Auckland, I bowled along last week to the Sheraton Hotel for a free lunch. It had something to do with PR. We all know this field serves an important function in modern society, and that you can always count on them for food. I was hungry. As such, I turned up at 12pm sharp, and was met by a woman from the Public Relations Institute of New Zealand. 'Nice to meet you,' I said. 'When's lunch?'

The event was sponsored by Corbans. Swigging on a bottle of Lion Red, I mooched in the hotel foyer waiting for the doors of the Tamaki Room to open, and eyed up the display stand for *Dancing with Beelzebub*, a thriller by former National Party MP and New Zealand First policy writer Michael Laws, who had been booked as guest speaker. There is always a price for a free lunch.

About 40 people were in attendance. Most were trouts of an uncertain age. Is there a special hand-to-hand combat class that is compulsory in the PR trade? Their speed at whipping out business cards was one thing, but their firm, athletic handshakes came as a shock. 'You've got big hands,' I winced at a woman whose fingers were so long that she shook my elbow. 'I'm German,' she said.

Finally we were granted admission, and I found myself sitting at the head table – I told you about my influence – beside some guy from Whitcoulls. Next to him was Laws. 'Nice to meet you,' I said. 'When's lunch?' No sooner had I spoken than a bloody big steaming plate of food arrived.

We're talking a herb and brioche-crusted rump of lamb on ratatouille of vegetables with a tarragon glaze. In short, it was lamb.

My God, what a feast! You'd have to walk a long day's march to find a better meal. The meat swooned to the touch; pink, tender, rumpish, it bleated 'Eat me!' with every prod, and acted the merry goat as it fell about in the sauce. Too right I filled my boots.

Delicious. Irritatingly, the Whitcoulls rep insisted on making conversation. 'I hope no one steals the book,' he fretted, casting a nervous eye towards the foyer. 'That's a bit on the highly unlikely side,' I replied. 'It's actually a very good book,' he sulked. Really? I read it while stretched out on my red velvet sofa at work a few days ago when no one had invited me to a free lunch. Set in Wanganui, *Dancing with Beelzebub* is a multi-murder mystery as well as a political intrigue. It doesn't make any sense, and near the end a National Party candidate is captured by a pair of crazed lesbians who tie him down and bugger him with a dildo. Michael Laws – clearly, he's got issues, but he's all right.

A number of colleagues asked me afterwards if he still wears eyeliner. This was a puerile question. It's enough to say that he wore a denim shirt and a mullet haircut. Windy, excitable, fit, he is an engaging fellow, with a dyslexic face – he is 42, but could pass for 24. He blathered knowledgeably about Gatt and foolishly about George Best. We got on like a house on fire, and fortunately dessert arrived just as I was about to ask him if he still wears eyeliner.

We're talking chilled grand marnier sabayon in a chocolate cup with seasonal fruit. Superb! The colours were a play of light and shadow, and I liked the way the sabayon turned to custard. It was sweet, and babyish, and genteel. I lapped at the thing like a hog.

Laws then got up and made a long speech about something. Afterwards, freshly brewed coffee and tea was served. Out in the foyer, the dutiful Whitcoulls man did a roaring trade, selling between 25 and 30 copies of *Dancing with Beelzebub* at $29.95 a pop. 'A compelling speech!' I congratulated Laws. 'Thanks, you too!' he said. He was a strange man.

Over drinks to a select audience, Laws set about solving the country's social ills, but was dragged away by his publisher to another appointment. A shame. Worse, Sheraton staff kicked us out of the Tamaki Room at 2.30pm. I had begun to hope the Institute might spring for a free dinner.

Only the truly disgraceful were left standing. 'I earn a lot of money, and I expect my kids to have a solid education!' barked a trout in pearls; 'I don't want my kids being taught by goddamned Commie-influenced schoolteachers!' railed an *Independent* journalist. Clearly, time to go. It was wet and filthy outdoors, a whole other New Zealand, costly, unfair, possibly overrun by crazed lesbians, more likely just waiting for its next meal.

21 August 1999

MILK, NO SUGAR

YES, AGAIN. This column's insistence on celebrating New Zealand tearooms is now in its third instalment in a series which may dribble on for quite some time. The cause is just, the intention is good: over the past 10 years, the rise of the espresso slophouse has driven honest, decent coffee lounges off the landscape, for the enjoyment of the boring few and the dismay of the honest, decent many. Enough is bloody well enough. Amazingly, and of course very pleasingly, the good news is that my ravings have the support of Julie Dalzell, publisher and editor of *Cuisine*, 'New Zealand's pre-eminent food magazine', as *North & South* recently hurrahed with its usual sunny manner.

'Whatever happened,' Dalzell pleads in her latest editorial, 'to the great Kiwi tradition of the lunch bar and the neighbourhood cake shop? The new metropolitan cafe society assaults our jaws on a daily basis with massive hunks of bad focaccia filled with indiscernible mixtures . . . In going forward with coffee the baristas in the city have replaced the cooks. I betcha most of them couldn't even knock up a decent Marmite and crisp iceberg lettuce sandwich, let alone a lamington – truly a thing of beauty. It's in the regions of heartland Kiwiland that "real lunch" food reigns.'

Well, all right! She shoots, she scores! But in congratulating Dalzell in coming to her senses, and jumping on board the band-wagon, serious questions need to be asked. Is she blind? The lunch bar and the neighbourhood cake shop remain alive and well in pretty much every urban suburb in New Zealand. Is she serious in believing that 'real lunch' exists only in that mythical geography known too cutely and patronisingly as the 'heartland'? I can vouch for good scoffs in three of the main centres – really, I should do something about organising a junket to Dunedin – and can also tell the dismal truth that I have occasionally swaggered into small towns and eaten shit.

Two more inquiries. Is there any such thing as 'good' focaccia? And what the hell does 'barista' mean? No doubt answers can be quickly found in another piece of literature which arrived on my desk at the same time as *Cuisine*. I refer to an appalling thing called *Wellington's Cafe Culture*, a 120-page guide to 52 cafes, which is possibly as pathetic and pretentious as a similar effort produced for Auckland cafes a few years ago. Compare and contrast. Articus on Symonds Street 'is like being backstage at a theatre, with that lingering sense of moments past and moments yet to come'; the Wellington abortion begins, 'This book is a map to the soul of Wellington City.' Thank you, good night, and would you please just die.

Back to more good news. Life, unpredictable and superb, has continued to skip my way in the shape of letters which recommend coffee lounges around New Zealand. A few weeks ago, I published numerous replies from readers on the subject; it has since prompted votes from Carolyn of Owaka, South Otago, for the **Lofts** in Balclutha ('Good chicken and cashew sandwiches'), and Cathy of Greenhithe, Auckland, for **Golden Sands** in Browns Bay ('It is the only place I can still find asparagus rolls'), and Trish of address unknown for **Joanola Tearooms** in Leeston ('The most outrageously well-stuffed filled rolls'). Someone with an illegible signature gave thanks to the **Empire Tearooms** in Dargaville, while **Lemons** in Hokowhitue Village, Palmerston North, received a formal notice from R. and J. Bell: 'As a couple who in our retirement move about New Zealand and frequently meet up with friends for lunch in our home city, we can commend Lemons as belonging among the best in the tearoom category.'

Cheers. Most excellently, I now have a roving correspondent. Robin of Marton wrote on behalf of **Harry's Cafe** in Whangarei, the **Copper Kettle** in her home town, and another Marton tearoom, **Hawkestone Gardens**, which coincidentally carries her address but will not be open until summer; she also mentioned that she regularly drives the length of the North Island, and announced, 'Your column has given me a mission. I shall screech to a halt at every likely looking bastion of the coffee pot, and report back.'

I have already written to Robin urging her to be true to her word. So far she has replied with warm remarks on the **Fudge Farm** at Maungataupere, and 'an odd place' in Awanui: 'It hasn't got glass ranch sliders yet, so when the weather is bad, the roller doors are down and it looks closed but IT'S NOT!' Interesting. So how the blazes do you get in? Squeeze underneath the door?

I await her next report with great interest. But I need more tips, more tearoomographies – I need a map to the rissoles of New Zealand, to the egg sandwiches and the coffee poured straight from the pot. Please, write in. I am offering an incentive, a reward. The best letter will receive $20 from my own pocket. Not much, I know. But it's enough to buy anyone a good, honest meal at their friendly neighbourhood coffee lounge.

17 July 1999

BRIDGE TO TE AROHA

BECAUSE IT was the Monday of Queen's Birthday, and because the day was warm, and because I had just finished reading *Journey Without Maps*, Graham Greene's classic 1938 account of his four-week, 350-mile – those were the days before the sickly kilometre – walk through Liberia, I got up and got the hell out of town last week. Inspired, ready, fizzing, the least I could do was get on a bus. I got on a bus. The 1.30pm took me to Paeroa.

Make that the 2pm. Greedily, the bus company had overbooked the passenger list, so we waited for 30 minutes while a back-up vehicle arrived. Snafu. It was up there with the behaviour of the woman who booked my ticket – sighing, bad-tempered, resolutely unhelpful. As a practised non-driver, I have come to expect shoddy treatment from both Newmans and InterCity. If you can, take the train, every time.

The right lane was choked with poor devils returning to Auckland. We arrived at Paeroa in the late afternoon. But the light was good for another 30 minutes, so I headed for a turn-off, marked by a bush where birds were squawking their close-of-day heads off. My mind was racing; my feet followed. I thumbed a lift with Doug, a hell of a nice bloke who teaches special needs in Hamilton, to a place which I now realised was exactly where I wanted to go.

Te Aroha – nestled beneath a mountain, pop. about 3,500, famous for its hot pools – is the most exquisitely pretty town I know of in New Zealand. It has a spell, a mystique. The air is soaked in soda from the underground mineral waters, bubbling up beneath Mt Te Aroha; the mountain looms, whiskered with toetoe, over the downhill town, the curling Waihou River, the friendly people.

I lived there in the summer of 1980. Make that a very brief summer. Sensibly, the *Te Aroha News* gave me the sack after four weeks. Such is the road which leads to the *Listener*, and back again . . . I booked a $58 room at the excellent Te Aroha Motel, where host Bill Smith gave me milk and cookies, and set off for a beer at the Grand Tavern. It was stuffed. Taxidermists had made the walls wild with impressive displays of fish, antlers, pigs' heads, and the jaws of a mako shark caught by Zeke Ellis. A woman walked in to update the board listing the weights for Fish of the Month.

Opposite PJ's burger bar, a bloke sat on the pavement licking a Trumpet, and said, 'No call for that!' A souped-up hoonmobile had just executed an absurdly loud wheelie in the middle of Whitaker Street. He was sensitive; he planned to open a shop devoted to cardboard exhibits. Cardboard? 'Boxes,' he enthused. Learnedly, he began detailing the 1920s period of cardboard box art. 'Come back when I've opened!' Absolutely.

By this time, I had enjoyed a soak inside a private wooden tub at Mokeno Pools, so warmed and loosened that I easily braved the brisk winter night in my shirtsleeves. I felt like strolling for hours. But when PJ's closed at 10pm, so did the town; a stranger ought not to be wandering the streets after dark.

First thing the next morning, I conquered Mt Te Aroha. On the mountain, the women come and go, talking of . . . the *Listener*. Strangely, I was taking a breather on a seat just as two women walked down, discussing the magazine's merits. They were both subscribers. Kate claimed to fondly remember me from 19 years ago. Were these women saints?

Later, I passed an old bloke with a handsome walking stick. He climbed to Bald Spur once a week. 'I have one pace. Dead slow, then stop,' he said. Good man. I followed his method to the summit, through dark, silent groves and patches of light, and looked across the great plain to Mt Ruapehu, Mt Ngauruhoe, Mt Taranaki, White Island, and possibly to Liberia.

Back down again, I had time for one more soak in the hot pools and a wander past the bowling green, the trees, the drinking fountain, before thumbing a lift with a Maori bloke, who played Black Uhuru on his car stereo and said he was studying landscape design. He dropped me off at Morrinsville, where I sat beside the tracks and waited to catch the 3.15pm train for home.

I was only passing through. Day tripper. I cannot report on the Te Aroha economy, its hopes, its dreams, or give any kind of blathering inspection, other than to remark on the quality of its hard winter light, the last of the autumn gold in the domain, the open faces on every corner, and say that it is the most exquisitely pretty town I know of in New Zealand.

19 June 1999

BARBECUE WEATHER

AT A NEARBY PARK, the paths are painted crimson with fallen Moreton Bay figs, round and small and soft, like plums, easy to squash underfoot, and they smell like sweet coconut. Inside, the flesh is dry in the centre, sticky at the edges; and their red skins blacken in the sun. They fall at the very end of barbecue weather.

I picked up about a dozen, and cradled them on top of a banana cake I had bought for $4 from a stall. 'Baked this morning,' said the woman, who sat in a deck chair in the shade. Another woman was selling books for $1 from a cardboard box. I bought the revised King James Bible. 'I don't know if that's the proper one,' she said. 'Religion isn't my field of expertise.'

It was early afternoon on a warm Saturday. I walked across the grass in my jandals, lay down beneath a California redwood, and turned to Leviticus.

'And these you shall have in abomination among the birds, they shall not be eaten, they are an abomination: the eagle, the vulture, the osprey, the kite, the falcon according to its kind, every raven according to its kind, the ostrich, the nighthawk, the seagull, the owl, the cormorant, the ibis, the water hen, the pelican, the carrion vulture, the stork, the heron according to its kind, the hoopoe, and the bat.'

What's a hoopoe?

Away from the small type and the thin, important pages, there was the usual bumbling Saturday scene being played out – an Asian woman standing in an upstairs window above a restaurant, a raffle to win a hamper of Easter eggs, a hippie on a bicycle. The sky was

31

completely and utterly blue, a pearler, and I got up to buy a cup of tea and an Afghan biscuit for $2, and then I lay down again.

'And these are unclean to you among the swarming things that swarm upon the earth: the weasel, the mouse, the great lizard according to its kind, the gecko, the land crocodile, the lizard, the sand lizard, and the chameleon.' And the camel, the hare, the swine, the rock badger, and 'whatever goes on its belly', and 'anything in the seas or the rivers that has no fins or scales'.

So I asked my wife to buy some sirloin. I already had four Hutton's Real Chicken Sizzlers left in the fridge from the previous night's barbecue, when my five-year-old godson and his parents came over, late as usual, which meant I finished cooking in my backyard in the dark. Later, while the adults were blathering, I took my godson outside and we put dry branches of December's Christmas tree onto the vague coals on the barbecue, and watched them catch fire, the flames shaking shadows all over our faces. 'I like coming to your house, Steve,' said Will.

I hadn't bothered to clean the ashes by Saturday afternoon. After a snizz on the couch, I waddled outside and piled on paper and pinecones, lit a match, and then walked around the creek at the back of my flat. It was at high tide, so the white-faced and presumably abominable herons were nowhere in sight. But the mullets – such an unfortunate name – were jumping out of the water, and their silver scales flashed in the low sun; and the eels looked good enough for Moses to eat. I watched the creek flow. Walking home towards the thin smoke wriggling into the air from my backyard, I saw two well-known lesbians, and the sunset had bathed their faces an interesting orange.

I threw some coals on the barbecue, changed into long pants, and watered the garden. My cat chased the hose. The phone rang: it was my oldest friend, a union official who lives in Sydney, back in the country for a week's holiday. He said, 'I'm going to go fishing tomorrow morning, but what are you doing after that?' I said, 'Mate, come over and I'll light up the barbecue.'

About 10 minutes before he called, I had placed the barbecue lid over the sirloin. It was now a perfectly cooked steak. I got the bottle of Wattie's tomato sauce, and my wife made some sort of green salad with mint sauce, and boiled a potato, and I put the Hutton's Real Chicken Sizzlers on the barbecue grill in case I got hungry later in the evening, and then I sat down at the garden table and filled my fat, dazed face. Delicious.

The sun had gone down in the west, over the silent mangroves and the creek that now shuffled back towards the bay, and a full moon was rising in the east. I had put the Moreton Bay figs in a bowl on the table just for their smell. It was black night by 8.23pm, and it was the last day of daylight saving, the last day of summer.

1 April 2000

AUTUMN

THIS IS NICE. The softer light, the cooler air, the sky that settles in for an early night: April is the tenderest month. It's true that Auckland doesn't do autumn very well. You really want the South Island, or riverside towns like Cambridge and Taihape, for the brittle colours, the fragile collapses. You want the smell of coal in Greymouth at dusk, the white sea at early morning in Mt Maunganui.

You want all the sadness of autumn. I love it. Age, and death, and love, and memory – it's like twilight all the time. A friend of mine hates twilight: it makes him depressed, anxious, powerless: you bet he loathes and detests autumn.

He needs a lot of company this time of year. Mostly I just laugh at his fears, pour him another drink, and sit by as he blathers away in a desperate attempt to combat the implacable silence of autumn. I'm not sure, but I think I know how he feels – a sense the next few months are like a trial separation, that life becomes an outline of something seen in the distance. Remote months, months like the end of an affair. 'Kill him so that he can feel he is dying,' as Caligula instructed.

Bring it on. You could say I was dying to see the dying of the summer light last weekend, when daylight saving closed its account, and autumn could officially get down to its melancholy business. I decided to leave town. All I might notice of the changing seasons in Auckland would be a bunch of style bores dressed in black on Saturday night, and black on Sunday night.

Where to go? My wife wanted to consult a map. All we had was a world atlas. Uruguay showed promise, and they say the Seychelles are pleasant this time of year. I rattled off a few rather more convenient destinations: Thames, Waihi, Helensville. Clearly, I was overexcited.

We ended up sailing on Saturday afternoon to Waiheke Island, where Jenny had arranged bed and breakfast at Appletree Cottage. Our hostess was Betty. She had lived on the island for 60 years, she said, and everyone knew her. I looked at her list of things to do. 'Sift compost. Chop firewood. Open oysters.' Could I help with anything? No, said Betty, she had a squadron of blokes on call: 'You just enjoy yourself, dear.'

Good idea. We had a lovely weekend. After dinner on Saturday night, we mooched along the beach, striped with the long shadows of dusk. It was summer's last shout – the kind of evening you never expect to grow old. I stuck a toetoe branch down the back of my neck. We found a green bug in much distress, upside down on the sand, and carried it inside a shell to the grass. Out in the water, a woman wearing a blue bikini jumped off the stern of a launch. There was a sickle moon.

Because the clocks were turned back an hour during the night, we got extra value for money at Appletree Cottage. Breakfast was leisurely. In the TV lounge, Betty listened to a choir on *Praise Be*: 'We will cling to the old rugged cross.' Then she talked about her garden, which was greatly enriched by elephant dung – she knew a man who owned a circus. She also talked about a man who tried to live in the watchhouse of a boat that had gone to ground on Blackpool beach, but 'he was taken away'.

Betty made and sold crafts. There were pussycat cushion covers (her own cat, Pamela, would turn 15 on Tuesday), and signs warning against piddling on the toilet seat. But by now the sky had opened wide, and was thoroughly blue.

Tremendous. We swam, we hoofed around to three different beaches, we wolfed down some bananas; perched on a rock, I read Boswell's *Life of Johnson*, while Jenny lay on the sand and filled her pretty head with Stephen Jay Gould.

Idyllic, casual, downright happy – where was melancholic autumn? It had to wait, arriving, inevitably, at dusk, which now began to fall, slowly and tenderly, collapsing the bright day, from about six that night.

We caught the boat back at 6.45pm. And that was how I saw the first dying of the light of autumn – at sea, the water turning black, the sky revealing a mess of stars. There was a chill in the air. Summer had flown the coop. It felt like something new was about to happen.

3 April 1999

THE BAKER'S DAUGHTER

A WOMAN called Jane wrote last week from my hometown of Mt Maunganui to ask whether she could borrow the giraffe's mask I modelled in a recent column. She wanted to attend a masquerade ball. Too right, I said, and stuffed the thing in a cardboard box and mailed it to her address. There was just no way I could refuse, because she had touched me with a reference to a certain bakery in the Mount.

I loved that bakery. The food was delicious to eat, and also to look at – I spent more time standing out on the pavement than inside, ogling through the thin lace window-curtain at the strapping doughnuts, and custard squares with egg all over their face, and slices of sponge cake bleeding with so much red, red jam that they looked like they had been in a road accident, and the way the harsh Mt Maunganui sunlight glistened on the white flakes of coconut sprinkled upon black, black lamingtons. A boy gets hungry. Heaven was a place where Jesus handed out sweets. But there was more than food at stake: the shop was owned by a woman whose daughter was in my class, and who I fell in love with.

She was gorgeous, although the only language I had to describe her then was pretty. She wore an alice band on top of her auburn hair. Her skin was pale, slightly blushing. She had eyes as big as doughnuts. She was a shy, quiet girl; a delicacy, sweet. All I remember about her clothes is that she wore a lot of white. I adored her soft, careful, musical voice. And she was a genius.

Like me, she was a nine-year-old in a classroom of 10-year-olds – we had been promoted because we were the smartest kids of our age. The same went in our advanced class. We were special. I suppose we were unbearable. Reading, writing, spelling, sums – how easy everything was. Life at school was all about certainties. The black woodstove in the corner of the room, the wallpapered exercise books, the raincoat on the peg, official recognition at assembly that my father had painted the swimming pool: you knew where you were, life was a matter of facts. When the baker's daughter got the highest marks, I followed; and the only other possibility is that when I got the highest marks, the baker's daughter followed. It was a simple arithmetic.

One day it was announced that two pupils were to represent Mt Maunganui in some kind of mastermind contest. A few dreamers in our class hoped they might be chosen – loud, brash, gauche girls, no doubt big-earning trouts these days – but of course the cut came down to me and the baker's daughter. We were packed off for the great day in the back of Miss Johnson's car, and travelled to the bustling urban centres of Te Puke, Katikati and Morrinsville. At each school, we were lined up on the assembly stage and competed in spelling and sums, as well as general knowledge. It was a cakewalk. We were unbeatable. Top boy and top girl in Te Puke, top boy and top girl in Katikati – you bet there was no sleep till Morrinsville.

Miss Johnson was our driver. She pulled into a reststop beside a river so we could eat our packed lunches, at which point the baker's daughter revealed three lamingtons. 'One each,' she said. It was the greatest sentence I had heard in my life. Was she Jesus? Most definitely, she looked beautiful that happy hour, her feet not touching the ground as she sat at the picnic table, and I'm sure she wore white socks and black plastic shoes.

People drive too fast. Miss Johnson got married later that year, and left town – she was always in a hurry. Speeding towards our final destination, I got carsick and vomited, mostly outside the car. Miss Johnson was sympathetic. The baker's daughter was not amused. At Morrinsville, I got carted off to the school's sickbay and missed the final show; rattled, the baker's daughter competed, and lost. Did she really say, 'Your fault'?

Things were never the same again between us. The next year, I discovered soccer, an immediate and profound calling which soon saw me relegated two divisions in the school streaming system. A jackass was born. I had to wait until I was 17 for my next academic honour, when some swine at the Ministry of Education scribbled a note on my University Entrance results saying my mark for maths, four percent, had broken the New Zealand record as a new low. The truly hopeless shame of it is that I had done my homework, and sweated through the three-hour exam attempting to answer every question.

To hell with scholarship. I just hope the baker's daughter is happy. She may have been intolerant of seeing her mother's lamington thrown up on the black, black tar, but she was a good person, lovely and intelligent, although the truth is that I was much more in love that year with an intense, black-haired girl in my class who wore lipstick on mufti day.

25 March 2000

OLD BOY

THERE IS a photo I like. There is a kid in it. He wears a pair of blue trunks and an outrageous hat, and he is playing with a toy car and sitting on the back steps of his house in Mt Maunganui. His hair is as white as a clean sheet: even his posture is admirable: life is as open as the hibiscus above his head. He is ready for anything. He is going to drive a big red truck across 18 continents, and wrestle a gorilla to the death all for the sake of a bunch of bananas, and enjoy a famous romance with an Arab princess before running off with her gold, and everything.

He must be about three or four. He seems a trusting fellow, a bit dim, not particularly active – nothing in the photo indicates he will ever get off his fat ass – and it's possible to detect a shyness about his features. But he's an ordinary New Zealand child, stripped for summer, healthy, well fed, his tiny little mind content to play with a toy car which is so basic that it must have come from inside a cereal packet.

He is fascinated by the strip of lawn that grows in the middle of the driveway. He learns to read by gawking at the sign in an arch above the garage door – JOHN BRAUNIAS, PAINTER AND WALLPAPERER. There is a goldfish pond in the front garden. Out the back, there is his second favourite word in the world – a chookhouse. In the kitchen, his mother throws away potato peel and vegetable stalks into something which is his favourite word in the world – a chookbucket. She says, 'Let's go and feed the chooks.' He doesn't have the faintest idea that chooks are the same thing as chickens, which you eat.

He knows where he lives – 143 Valley Rd, Mt Maunganui, Bay of Plenty, New Zealand, The World – but it confuses him that New Zealand is a couple of smudges on the bottom right-hand corner of maps, like it's nearly been forgotten and hardly matters. He has an Uncle Karl – not a real uncle, like Uncle Homer, married to his mother's sister, Auntie Winkie – who says to him, 'Ach! There you are, Fritz!' He likes being called Fritz by Uncle Karl, who steers ships to the shores of 18 distant continents.

His father has a strange accent. His mother wears an apron. He has lots of brothers and one sister. Everyone in the world is older than him. It's always hot. There is a round hole in the concrete porch where you stick the pole of a beach umbrella. It's a very deep hole, which goes under the earth, and a brutal, murderous troll lives down there – this is a well-known fact, common knowledge. The spike at the end of the umbrella pole will go right through the troll's head, and kill him, which is justice.

He talks all day. He can watch bugs crawl in the dirt for hours. His brothers lift him onto the clothesline, tell him to hold on, and then twirl it around and around. He can read. He knows all about trolls, and gorillas, and Arab princesses, and he does not like the thought of a whole town being invaded by a plague of rats – there is no Pied Piper, there are only rats. He writes letters of the alphabet – mostly, S, T, E, V, E; he is an egomaniac – at the bottom of the driveway with rocks. He climbs onto the garage roof and looks at the top of Mt Maunganui, and his head is full of schemings and imaginings, journeys and idiotic dramas . . .

The photo was taken sometime last century. This column, as usual, is written at home on a Monday night after work. Tomorrow, 20 June, is my birthday – hi, my name's Steve, I'm a Gemini – and I turn officially really old. It's one of those ages that you reach with a zero tacked on solemnly at the end. 20. 30. Something like that.

An old fool, an old coot. An old guy who is so startled and deeply afraid of his advanced years that he looks at a photo taken when he was three or four, and tries to remember that grinning innocent in the hat and trunks.

Well, I always get morose on the eve of 20 June. This year – it's that zero at the end of my new age, clanging like a slow bell – should have felt even worse. A chance to reflect on time past, but also to think about the coming terrors of what is drearily known as middle age – desertion, madness, poverty, ill-health, a sad and pathetic urge to wear funky clothes. The scrap-heap, the boarding house. At best, a weekly 150-word column in the Golden Showers retirement village newsletter.

Incredibly and rather embarassingly, though, this column has taken nine hours to write – nine hours of blundering away at commas, dashes, semicolons, exclamations, brackets, the whole nine slow yards of what it takes to form a sentence. It's now 2.56am, 20 June, and there you have it: no time left to wallow: happy birthday, already.

1 July 2000

LEPIDOPTERA

AS A SOUVENIR of the week I once spent mooching around on holiday in Kuala Lumpur, I got my mother a present – a mounted butterfly, *Trogonoptera brookiana albescens*, or Rajah Brooke's Birdwing. I loved it at once. Vast and delicate, the male specimen was obviously quite dead but its emerald stripes still glowed and dazzled against its black wings. I wrapped its glass case in newspapers and carried it back via a few days in Perth to my mum's home in Mt Maunganui.

The butterfly was first discovered and named by the great English botanist Alfred Wallace. I had never heard of him until a few weeks ago, on a hot summer's night when I couldn't get to sleep, and got up to read my wife's copy of his 1853 book, *Travels on the Amazon* – in a recent column, I mentioned his perfect, shimmering sentence, 'I missed my toucan.'

The book hardly passes as a classic. He gets dysentery, and 'evacuates slime and blood'; he casually remarks that some poor devil dies in agony after eating dirt; he catches monkeys, eels and parrots; he drones, 'I was now in the country of the painted turtle and the white umbrella-bird.' His writing seems without any real purpose. Maybe he was in deep trauma.

He had spent four years in the tropics finding specimens he could sell to museums and private collectors. In the final chapter, he tells how he is about to sail home to England. 'I was reading in the cabin, when the captain came down and said to me, "I'm afraid the ship's on fire; come and see what you think of it."' Soon, the entire 35-ton brig is a raging inferno. The ship is abandoned, boats are lowered. 'I got my watch and a small tin box containing some shirts and a couple of old note-books . . . I did not care to venture down again, and in fact felt a kind of apathy about saving anything, that I can now hardly account for.' He loses everything. His insects, his plants, his monkeys, the lot. Four years of work really does go up in smoke. And there the book ends.

Further reading, as they say, was required. I looked up records of his life. Wallace came from a poor family. At 13 he was put to work, as a surveyor; his childhood interest in nature – 'I thought how nice it must be to know the names of rare plants when you find them' – was later excited in a serious way by a friend, Henry Bates. Together, they left for the Amazon. Wallace was 23.

After that expedition ended in flames, he took off again, this time to South-east Asia, assisted by Charles, the 16-year-old son of a London carpenter. He travelled for eight years, and collected 125,600 specimens. 28 May 1854: 'Return from the jungle and change clothes to sit down to kill and pin insects . . . I do not trust Charles yet with beetles.'

Four years later, bed-ridden in Malaya with a fever that gave him hot and cold fits, he turned over in his delirious mind the 'great problem of the origin of the species . . . It suddenly flashed upon me . . . that only the fittest would survive.' He sweated out the fever for two more days and then wrote his thoughts in a letter to Charles Darwin. I suppose you could quite easily remark that it changed the world.

Darwin had worked on the theory of evolution since returning from the *Beagle* in 1836. His proposed book on the subject was still nowhere near finished when Wallace's letter shook him out of the trees. Astonished that someone else had stumbled upon the same central, devastating fact, he raced to publish *The Origin of Species* in 1859.

It was another fire, worse than the first. Wallace has become the forgotten man of natural history. With incredible good manners, he remained amiable while Darwin took the glory; returning to England, he made a packet from selling his collections, but invested badly, and was forced to mark Civil Service exam papers. He accepted a 500 pound wager to disprove that the earth was flat; his crackpot opponent refused to believe a word of Wallace's argument, hounded him through the courts and wrote a foaming letter to Wallace's wife: 'If your infernal thief of a husband is brought home some day with every bone in his head smashed to a pulp, you will know the reason.' Wallace became a socialist who believed in the after-life, preached the virtues of vegetarianism while continuing to eat meat, and liked to potter about in his conservatory, where he grew mainly native plants from Australia and New Zealand.

As for Rajah Brooke's Birdwing – Wallace named the lepidoptera in 1855 after English trader and adventurer Sir James Brooke, the so-called 'White Rajah' of Sarawak, whose rule was courtesy of the Sultan of Brunei. According to legend, and sales blather, the butterfly is thought to contain the White Rajah's soul. The price of his soul in the male specimen I bought probably only cost about $10 or $20.

After my mother died, I took her collection of souvenir tea-spoons, an electric heater, a table, a chair, some potplants, seashells she found on the beach, a sugar bowl, a cheap painting of a vase, and the glass case containing *Trogonoptera brookiana albescens*.

24 February 2001

CORRESPONDENCE

ALL COLUMNISTS receive mail. It's the best thing about this job. I adore the well-hung size of my manila folders marked *Correspondence*. And the brilliant thing about writing for the *Listener* is that strangers from all around the country take the time and effort to call you a piece of shit. But most people are really nice. The first reader to write in since I started this column was Graham from Taranaki. His charming postcard with Elvis on the cover came after my third column, and I have to admit that I still think: what was wrong with the first two?

Such monstrous egotism is provoked by the letters I have received in the post since 1999. They have arrived from the old, the young, the mad and the occasionally famous. Men, women and someone from Te Kuiti who claimed to be a cat. Exiles in Japan, Australia, Africa and England have written; and so has a terrific pest from Paraparaumu, on six or seven occasions, who remembers columns I wrote in *Metro* dating back to 1997 and can quote those ancient lines in his fantastic campaign to prove that I am a piece of shit. None of his letters are ever published. And still he keeps writing, his letterhead preposterously advertising himself as a 'Public Policy Researcher', with his withering asides and his strangled bleatings.

As a hog for praise, how much better it is to read Isobel from Whangamata telling me she inflicts my columns on her Bursary English class. Poor devils. 'You are a miracle from God,' emailed Alison, but it's likely her judgement was terribly impaired, because she later wrote saying my columns were 'almost better than sex'. Lindsay, the national director of Student Job Search, reckoned he used to work with me, and wrote, 'I'm looking for a publisher for my autobiography entitled *I Knew Steve Braunias*.' Iain of Kelburn wondered if there was a Steve Braunias fan club. No, but I'll accept donations in the meantime. Amanda of Wellington claimed, 'I'll have you know you would be on my list of top six dinner guests.' I hate dinner parties. I have a great reluctance about TV, too, but it was nice of Tim to email, 'Could you look for a job at 7.00pm on any channel. There are thousands of us who'd watch it.' Is that all?

No one has sent me flowers, but I very much appreciated John Hawkesby mailing me a $5 note, and there have been comp tickets to the Te Aroha spa pools, a voucher for the Tahuna Beach Holiday Park mini-golf course in Nelson, and an invite to a party at RD2 Bickerstaffe Road, Maungaturoto. A number of readers were kind enough to try to bring me closer to Jesus. Margaret of Lower Hutt enclosed a religious tract: 'I knew that after reading your articles I was being asked to send you this . . . You have been chosen, and I know not why!' Me neither. Didn't read it. Letters from well-meaning Christians are inevitable. So are letters from the easily offended. After the magazine published a column about sodomy, there were letters from J.D. of Pinehaven ('In my opinion, and the opinion of others I have shown it to, it is sick, tasteless and revolting'), P.C. of Ohope ('Totally unacceptable . . . appallingly unsuitable . . . I will not be renewing my subscription'), R.S. of Castor Bay ('I could not believe that a family magazine could publish such crudity . . . The demise of the *Listener* is inevitable'), Dennis of Taradale ('Grubby . . . inappropriate . . . I would suggest Steve Braunias be given a lengthy sabbatical without pay to enable him to clean up his mind') and R.E., also of Taradale ('What garbage . . . filth . . . Can you give me a reasonable explanation not to cancel my subscription?'). Sue of Christchurch seemed the most indigested: 'I hope I am one of thousands writing to express shock and disgust

. . . My partner and our 17-year-old son were equally gobsmacked . . . We are not the slightest bit prudish.' She suggested I send my pay that week to RISK, the Rape and Incest Survivors Collective, 'who work with survivors of the deed that he so callously narrated'.

Oh dear. Andrew of Housing New Zealand brought some consolation with his email: 'I attended a formal New Year's Day dinner at Lake Ohau Lodge. We were all required to give speeches. I told your joke and brought the house down and effectively ended the speaking as no one thought they could top it.'

As a sensitive soul, it was touching to receive poems from Warwick of Nelson, Jeffrey of Greymouth and Clare of Coromandel, which rather brilliantly rhymed 'Braunias' with 'genius'. Dorothy of Motueka sent me Ruth Dallas's classic 'Milking Before Dawn' poem ('Spring', page 129), and Barbara of Wellington mailed a copy of Elizabeth Bishop's poem 'One Art' ('The art of losing isn't hard to master') after I had publically whined about losing my cellphone for the sixth time. Alice of Taupo wrote a three-page sarcastic epic called 'Steve Braunias's Next Lamington'. It was rubbish. Far better were the lyrics of a song emailed by an anonymous 17-year-old of Tokoroa in response to my 'Hate' columns. It was called 'Love to Hate', and included this catchy refrain: 'I hate this I hate that I hate a lot of things/ And what I really, really hate is all the joy hate brings.'

As for the famous, both Keri Hulme and Brian Edwards wrote forgiving notes, and a learned letter about mangroves from Neva of Mongonui ended with the superb line, 'I am John Clarke's mum.'

I often hear from complete nobodies leading famous lives. An email from a guy whose name is best left unsaid blathered on for no apparent reason about his romance with a '21-year-old stripclub dancer and pseudo weird sex fiend'. John of address best left unsaid had read my comments on New Zealand mercenary Gayle Rivers

('Remains', page 50), and remarked, 'Last year I got instructions on weapons like the Stinger and Mistral anti-aircraft missiles, the AT4 and Dragon anti-tank missiles . . . I trained alongside the first SAS recruits and sang the parachutists song with them: "His parachute did not open, and they scraped him from the runway with a spoon."'

Mrs Brown of Taupo supplied an excellent recipe for pukeko, Mike of Wellington recommended a .177 BSA Meteor air rifle to kill rats, Jane's email mentioned she was pregnant and suffering from hyperemisis. The lives of people are endlessly fascinating. Well, except mine, according to Steve, whose email was blunt and to the point: 'Your banal and self-indulgent life does not merit having a weekly column written about it.' Quite right. I think I conceded his point in between the lines of my reply: 'Please, go fuck yourself.'

Thanks to everyone who has ever written in. Most of all to Katy of Palmerston North, who wrote from the house legendary *Listener* editor Monte Holcroft used to live in, and poured on the praise ('I need you to know I turn your words over in my head and in my mouth') to the extent that she made the effort to count 116 words in the final sentence of one of my columns ('Fairlie', page 77); and to Rosemary of Whakatane, who scribbled upset comments ('In poor taste . . . Boring and irrelevant . . . It is the little courtesies in life that count . . . I must have lost my sense of humour') on a ripped-out copy of my 'This Sporting Life' column (page 157), and repeated the act a few days later. Same column, different copy, roughly the same remarks written in the margins with the same blue pen. Cheers, Rosemary. No other correspondent has paid me the compliment of buying two copies of the *Listener* in the same week.

REMAINS

THERE IS A photo I like. It has four people in it. They are standing outside a building, and you are forced to look below the belt, at the bearded wallah wearing socks with sandals, the old codger with bow legs just waiting to sit astride a horse, the young fox dolled up in a miniskirt, the young dude wearing outrageous checkered trunks – strange how legs say so much about a summer's day in New Zealand. The date is February 1971. The place is revealed in the reflection in the window, where you can see the dense, sloping line of the hills above Greymouth. Our finest regional painters would kill for such an image. It comes from *A Geologist Remembers: Recollections of Fieldwork*, by Max Gage and Simon Nathan, and their book very nearly fell through the cracks of this magazine.

We recently held our annual clear-out of books deemed unsuitable or unreadable for review. Staff raided a table in the writers' room and took away all sorts of garbage. When the dust settled, I got up off my fat ass from the red velvet couch in my office – work here is often flat out – and ambled over to survey what was left behind. No one wanted *A Geologist Remembers*.

It was a sad sight, but then unwanted books always crush my feelings. Pity and rage leave me short of breath whenever I poke my snoot into a second-hand bookshop and notice perfectly good publications existing only to take up room. The worst case are the three Johns whose work can be found cluttering up every New Zealand second-hand store – John Braine, John Wain and John O'Hara. For years I bought their novels simply because they had become such lost souls. I wanted to save them from dust, and rot, and embarrassment. I gave them a good home.

As for *A Geologist Remembers*, it's worth it for more than just the priceless 1971 photo of the Greymouth staff of the New Zealand Geological Society. It stands as a nifty, affectionate memoir of Gage's 1936–47 stint with the society. He traverses creeks and ridges during a dusty summer in Porangahau, where he meets his wife: 'Just how and why it was that getting to know Molly Rose would break down my chronic shyness with girls, even girl students, is probably clear enough to those who know her.' Later, he goes out mapping among the Paleozoic rocks of Reefton, and listens to Bing Crosby gramophone records in a godforsaken hut.

He becomes a Coaster. Hail, thunder, sandflies, wet firewood, skewering rats with a carving knife, killing a trout with a geological hammer, a brawl in an abandoned hut ('Bill, bloodied and in a rage, came out with the rifle, whereupon Tom vanished into the bush'), the packhorse which fell off the steep Boatmans Creek track and landed on its feet on a ledge . . . Great days, vividly told. Top book.

Also neglected from our clear-out was Sheridan Gundry's *Isolated Lines: A history of electricity supply in Poverty Bay*. Yes. But even here are buried narratives, hints of how profoundly our century has changed, faint markings of the story of New Zealand. We hear of engineer Wally Neilsen who was given a full Masonic funeral, meter reader Jock Beattie who wore silk suits, and a woman called Shayne. In 1964, a 50,000-volt current transformer blew up, and covered Ron Turbitt in flames and scalding oil. In April 1952, power restrictions meant playing the radio was totally prohibited. The fact that electricity could be so quiet was awesome: 'Riding home at dusk when we were connected to the power in the late 1960s,' recalls Tikitiki farmer Ernest Ford, 'it often struck me as eerie to see the lights on in the houses but for all to be silent. It was the silence of it all that seemed so strange.' Nicely put, Tikitiki Ernie Ford.

You never know your luck in a remainder bin. Still the very best book I have rescued is *The Teheran Contract*, by Gayle Rivers, dumped in a 10-cent pile by my local library. It ought to be a New Zealand classic. 'I had made a habit of looking out for myself since I was a kid in New Zealand, hunting alone in the mountains with a small-bore rifle,' writes Rivers, before detailing his incredible mission as a solider of fortune to lead a crack strike force of mercenaries into Iran, and smuggle out three wealthy Jews placed on the death list of the PLO and Ayatollah Khomeini.

I'm tempted to say it must be fiction, except Rivers might steal into my house one night and choose one of 17 secret methods to kill me with his bare hands in 0.4 seconds. The drama is fantastic. The tension pounds in your ears. A lot of people get annihilated. But there is also the authentic voice of shameful New Zealand: 'I have a phobia,' Rivers confesses, 'about dying in my underwear.'

30 October 1999

MAN WITH THE GOLDEN SOUFFLÉ

SHOW ME A new New Zealand novel, and just you try and catch me as I head for the hills. I do not believe the glowing reviews, which I often headline in the *Listener* each week, for a moment. I'd much rather read – you know how it is – something good. But I recently snaffled a spy novel set in Wellington, *The Alpha Trip*, published in 1969 by Whitcombe and Tombs, and came away feeling that I had quite possibly stumbled upon a lost New Zealand classic. I read it last weekend. I was right. It's completely mad.

The distance of 30 years helps: the Wellington that Graham Billing describes seems so strange, so foreign: in fact, his New Zealand has a fuzzy, flickering tone, like old black-and-white film. One bloke talks about the public demand for colour TV – 'We can't go on much longer without it.'

The book's gloomy hero is Hugh Strachan. We know he is gloomy because Billing tells us, 'In general he could no longer see an important point to human life and endeavour.' He writes secret government reports for something called the Department of Co-Ordination Planning. Mostly, he's worried about the US Airforce military base at Woodbourne, near Blenheim. Then he gets seduced by a couple of hot Communist wenches. Talk about a honeytrap: one of the women, who is also a New Age nut, heals his sore back by stinging him with bees. Both of these Reds in his bed belong to a bunch of international Commies, who slip into the country disguised as film-makers. They hire him as a production assistant, and hoof out to Makara to film an opera for kids, *The Magic Hammer* (apparently based on a real film made by Geoff Murphy.)

Woodbourne, they tell him, sends coded information to nuclear ships, and their intention is to bring it down.

Cool. There is an exciting car chase that ends at Karori cemetery, and a vivid atmospheric scene where Strachan steals through the wharves at night taking surveillance photos of the American Embassy. There are plenty of nice domestic touches, too – Strachan reads 'The Wizard of Id' comicstrip in the *Dominion*, drives a Sunbeam Stiletto, feeds pigeons, drinks at the Midland Hotel. The guy also has a keen fetish for women's clothing: 'She wore black leotards and a scarlet blouse with a tumbling ruffled Restoration gentleman's lace front . . . She wore a plain black velvet hostess skirt and vermilion ceramic ear-rings set off her blouse . . . On the floor was a wisp of black bra and petite black panties caught with petals of white lace on each thigh . . . '

But what really gets *The Alpha Trip* slobbering with pleasure is food. There is more food in this book than food in your fridge. It is the Great New Zealand Food Novel. We know Strachan likes cooking because Billing tell us in the first few pages, 'Strachan liked cooking.' Immediately we are given a recipe for beef curry: 'He always thickened the sauce with a potato sliced very thinly so that it cooked into a paste and he always added a little finely chopped lemon peel with the slivers of porterhouse beef.' Strachan also dines out: 'At the Jolly Frog they ate avocados, sole meunière, chateaubriand, and chilled fresh strawberries with rich cream and a spoonful of kirsch.' He whips up a soufflé ('"Do you have any honey," he asked suddenly'), serves a burglar some breakfast ('The eggs would take exactly four and a half minutes to be firm but soft in the white and runny but hot in the yolk'), and drools as one of the Reds slaves over a hot stove ('She coated the chicken pieces in egg and breadcrumbs and fried them slowly in a quantity of butter to which the herbs were added.') It goes on (lobster salad), and on (pancakes with bacon), and on (a chase scene ending at the Lariat Steak Bar), with incredible attention to detail, told in a flat, monotonous, hungry tone – food is a serious business in *The Alpha Trip*, and the effect is somehow profound.

But what did critics make of Billing's art? Writing in *Comment: A New Zealand Quarterly Review*, Harry Orsman poured shit on *The Alpha Trip* from a great, smirking height. He tore it to shreds. 'Thin . . . ludicrous . . . misinformed . . . trivial . . . pedantic . . . ' Worst of all, he attacked the 'rather tasteless recipes'.

Orsman owes Billing an apology, or some such synonym he can no doubt easily find in one of those pedantic New Zealand dictionaries which he edits, and which earn such glowing reviews. *The Alpha Trip* is one hell of a read. True, for much of the time, it's exactly like Strachan's dog Nicola – barking. That outrageous conspiracy theory of secret US military involvement at Woodbourne! What was Billing on about there? In real life, there was absolutely nothing to fear. The government and the media told us so.

At the time, Prime Minister Keith Holyoake and his deputy Jack Marshall assured the public that Woodbourne 'monitored aerospace disturbances'. Quite right, said the press. *New Zealand Herald*, 1 February 1971: 'Twelve journalists inspected Woodbourne on Saturday and came away convinced there is nothing sinister.'

In 1994, a declassified US State Department telegram revealed this was a deliberate cover-up. Woodbourne was in fact used to monitor atmospheric nuclear testing.

28 October 2000

WAS

BECAUSE CHILDREN never tidy up after themselves, I recently took it into my hands to restore some order in the *Listener* writers' room. This led to our annual massive clearance giveaway of books deemed unsuitable for review. Rows of them were dumped on the floor outside my office. Swiftly, steadily did staff stoop and swoop; and just like last year, I waited until the dust was settled before making my move.

No one had wanted the *Enderby Settlement Diaries* (Wild Press, $60). A shame. This is a handsome book, dealing with an obscure and dismal paragraph in New Zealand history – the failed 1849–52 colony of Auckland Island, which is nowhere near Auckland, but is in fact below Stewart Island and just up the road from Antarctica. 'Almost certainly the smallest, shortest-lived and most remote of all British colonies,' according to the book's editors, it was leased by the Southern Whale Fishery Company and thought ideal to advance the cause of British whaling in the South Pacific.

It flopped. Two of the company's senior officers, William Mackworth and William Munce, recorded the unfortunate experiment in their diaries, published here for the first time. What a miserable existence it was. 'Strong gales . . . severe gales . . . heavy gales . . . brisk gales . . . weather very boisterous.' Someone keeps thieving company firewood: 'I have hopes of discovering the rogue'. Long days plod by without excitement: 'Friday November 15. Sent Bromley off for the sheep.'

All that wind and isolation tearing at the nerves . . . Enderby, who installs himself as lieutenant governor, seems to lose his mind, and threatens to shoot anyone trying to remove him from residence. At midnight on 14 October 1850, Miss Hallett fires a rifle at her brother, the chief medical officer, and then (love the spelling) 'leasurely reloaded the gun and shot herself . . . The side of this unfortunate person's head fearfully lacerated'.

True, there was a measure of gaiety on the island's 4 December anniversary, when a public holiday and regatta were held. Also, Governor Grey pokes his snoot into harbour – for two days. Intolerably, though, Mackworth puts a stop to the sale 'of all wine and spirituous liquor'. The more agreeable Munce reads *The Adventures of a Thug*, and records the happy news that 'I opened one of my cases and took out two bottles of brandy'.

Successful hunts of the leviathan were too rare for good business. In the first year, 30,000 pounds had been spent on the colony, and only 3,000 quid put back. When they finally pack it up, Mackworth admits, 'Everyone in this place has been longing to leave it from the time of his arrival and endeavouring by every opportunity to do so.'

Such a vivid, depressing read. *Unofficial Channels* (Victoria University Press, $50), another of my rescues, is more worldly. It collects the personal letters sent between New Zealand foreign affairs diplomat Alister McIntosh and three of his staff, Foss Shanahan, George Laking and Frank Corner, from 1943–66. The hum of crucial political events – Suez, Vietnam, Rhodesia, the Cold War – plays in the background. And so there is the occasional *Mission: Impossible* riff: 'I hope you will destroy this note as soon as you have absorbed its contents.' There is also a low rumble that New Zealand is content to be a stooge to American foreign policy. But for the most part, the soundtrack has the kind of laughter from *Yes, Minister*.

How the diplomats shake their heads at the fools voted into

power. Prime Minister Walter Nash is cast as a wild card; after his meeting with Kruschev, 'He said things in public which if reported back to New Zealand will finish the Labour Party.' External Affairs Minister John Doidge, and his wife, receive this splendid dismissal: 'I have always felt that Doidge had the ruins of an intelligence . . . Mrs Doidge is an extremely nice person but completely bemused, and out of this world.'

The biggest knockabout farce is Holyoake's decision not to send a representative to JFK's funeral. 'The PM frankly hooted at the idea of anybody going from New Zealand on the score of expense and fuss.' The press pour scorn on the titanic lack of tact; Holyoake desperately tries to find a spare cabinet minister to attend the blasted funeral, but finds only 'Mr Gossman, who refuses to travel by air'; after that, anyone will do, but 'the last available plane had gone'.

Finally, a book of the dead. Errol W. Martyn's detailed and thorough *For Your Tomorrow* (PO Box 1521, Christchurch, $44.95) is subtitled, 'A record of New Zealanders who have died while serving with the RNZAF and Allied Air Services from 1915–42.' There are two more volumes to come, 'detailing losses from 1943 onward'. An attached release notes the author has 'an interest in casualties'.

Yes. There are some 4,800 accounts of courage and agony, accident and death. Collided with Sopwith Camel. Died from typhoid fever. Shot down by a nightfighter. Died of a heart attack while marching down to the docks. Attacked by 12 fighters. Lost without trace. Did not survive incarceration. Died when the ship transporting him back to Japan was torpedoed and sunk by an American submarine. Attacked by three Fokkers. Walked into spinning propellor . . . The litany of New Zealand casualties begins on 30 July 1915, and it probably never ends.

3 February 2001

WINTER

AROUND THE CORNER from my office is a view that funnels down a suburban street towards a bay. Framed by trees and houses, it's a tight, cropped picture, like the corner of a postcard, showing a patch of water beyond a seawall. There's always one boat parked in it. I love looking at that glimpse, that ripped sudden image, which six months ago seemed so bright and childish in summer, and two months ago was exactly like the kind of sadness you expect of autumn, and now – this afternoon, walking home from work – has winter's hard lines.

Fantastic. Winter is case closed, roll credits, the end. A dramatic bore might go further and say the boat in the bay is manned by Charon, death's ferryman, about to punt his cargo of the dead to an unmarked shore. Really, it doesn't look that bad. It's only a small boat. You could reach out and put it in your pocket, and it would feel cold and wet, like a shell.

I wish it did look more crucial, more disheartening. But winter hasn't got off the ground where I live. There is still too much life. Winter is late. It's been delayed. It goes through the motions: trees are stripped bare, their branches as bald as bones, and the days are shorter, it gets dark at 4pm, you can smell coal at twilight, boats and fences and telephone poles have hard lines, the cat needs his sleep, some soup would be nice, there's always someone who hogs the electric heater, getting out of bed in the morning confirms your suspicion that work is a sham, etc.

Yes. But the sky is too often blue, and what I really want is stink weather. Lashings of rain. Darkness at 11am. Frosts, and the wind that you get in Greymouth, the one they call the Barber, which slices along the Grey River and is so sharp that it can cure any hangover known to man. Or a proper Wellington southerly, like the one whacking Athletic Park last weekend when the All Blacks played France – a mate watched it on TV, and said the scene was something out of the 1950s. An old-fashioned cold.

Bring it on. I can take it. Has the iceskating rink in Fairlie frozen up yet? Is the Desert Road closed, as it is every winter, when the TV news shows a reporter wearing a nice coat with a hood on it, telling Judy or Carol that motorists should be careful? That's the story. Auckland – it's too damned soft.

We need winter. It makes us, sorts us out. The greatest single chapter in New Zealand fiction – apologies for being male about these things – remains Johnson's hideout in the bush, in *Man Alone* by John Mulgan. 'Life in the Kaimanawas, while winter lay over them, wasn't dull, it was too uncomfortable to be dull. Later, when he became weak with exposure and lack of food, there came on him a settled apathy which stopped him from feeling the conditions in which he lived, but this was not dullness; it was a sickness against which he had to fight.'

True, a winter like that is pushing things a bit far for my blood. I'll settle for a city winter. The kind that traps office workers to the point where they begin to simmer with exaggerated resentments and insane revenge fantasies against their colleagues. They stare outside the window, and see merciless rain, howling winds: they develop cabin fever, there is no escape: life seems unfair, narrow, appalling: they are sick of the sight and the idiotic existence of each other. Normal apathy is perverted into abnormal rage. The boss is revealed as a jackass. Lust will demand release. Injustice lurks behind every wall divider, despair blocks the doors. Someone – the suspense, the neurotic speculations! – is about to lose it, big-time.

The great indoors. But the slowness of a wet week has such promise. Forced inside, the body closes down, and we learn to think. In summer, sunshine skips along, naive and almost Christian, a do-gooder, never counting the hours, while winter concentrates the mind. And so the potential for madness, but also intellectual discovery, erotic seizures (winter is the time of flame), emotional commitments. The strong shall survive.

All this is winter as it should be. It wants to pick a fight. Heartless, profound, desolate, the loneliest, most harrowing time of year, a stern and resolute authority, sick of living. The kind of winter that sounds the hard, clanging bell, and we all hear it, we all know what it means.

10 July 1999

DEAD MAN TALKING

IN JANUARY 1997, the *Listener* sent me to Wellington, because I had lined up three interviews. I talked to Kevin Milne of *Fair Go* outside the Avalon studios, next to the shattered remains of Eion Scarrow's old *Dig This* glasshouse. I met National Radio's Mike Hosking on Parliament's front lawn. The third person I interviewed was Justin Fashanu.

I wanted to meet Fashanu because we don't get too many big, black, British, furiously Christian, sometimes openly and other times furtively gay, ex-professional footballers in these parts. He was here to play for Miramar in New Zealand's summer league. His agent established a few rules – do *not* ask about Fashanu's claims that he once had an affair with Julie Goodyear from *Coronation Street*, do *not* ask about Fashanu's claims that he once had a lot of affairs with high-ranking politicians in John Major's government. Those revelations were for a price.

I met Fashanu for lunch on Willis Street. He was an astonishing sight in pale Wellington – large, beaming, obviously famous; also, he was beautifully tailored, and his manners were exquisite. He was kind, and considerate. He listened. He was sensitive. He tried so hard to please, to convince. There was some sort of profound struggle going on to declare himself, to work something out, to find the right word, the right path, the right way of being. He wanted to make sense of his past – the scandals, the failures. He was exhausting and bewildering company, one of the strangest people I had ever met. He said he felt good. He looked good. He breathed in God; he wanted to be a good Christian. He was hopeful. He gave advice. He talked a lot about his future.

On 2 May the next year, his body was found in a lock-up garage in Shoreditch, London. Fashanu had hanged himself. He was 37.

Last week, I received a fax from Colin McNamee. The guy has a fabulous address: Ivy Cottage, Castle Bolton. He said he was writing a book about Fashanu, that he had read my *Listener* article, and could I provide him with anything further? I tape all my interviews, but never keep the cassettes. But I looked in a drawer at home and found a tape marked 'Fashanu'.

We had talked for an hour. Colin said it was the last substantial interview Fashanu gave before his death.

Fashanu is a 'story'. He was fostered out with his younger brother John. Both became celebrated footballers. Justin represented England Youth, and England Under-21. In 1980, playing for Norwich, he scored a goal against Liverpool – a brilliant goal, an outrage, blinding, a goal that still electrocutes. In his book *Football in Sun and Shadow*, Eduardo Galeano writes about a goal by Bobby Charlton: 'The ball obeyed him. She travelled the field following his instructions and flew into the net before he even kicked her.' It was a goal like that, scored by a black man in a yellow shirt.

It made Fashanu famous. A year later, he became the first black one million pound footballer, transferred to Nottingham Forest. He lasted one season – 31 games, three goals, a waste of money. The remainder of his career was a map leading nowhere. He played for an English club called Leatherhead. He travelled to America, where all clubs have terrible names – he played for Atlanta Ruckus.

And he came out that he was gay, and his brother John never spoke to him again. He sold 'torrid' stories about his affairs. He ran a gay bar in Canada, and found God in America. And then to Miramar, and then, in 1998, back to Atlanta, where a 17-year-old accused him of sexual assault. A month later, back in England,

Fashanu went to Chariots Roman Spa (the *Sun*: 'where he indulged in a final orgy of homosexual lust'), showered, shaved, and walked across the road, where he broke into a garage and hanged himself from the rafters. Police found a suicide note saying he had consensual sex with his accuser, but was being blackmailed.

The brother, that goal, Bet Lynch, his childhood, his God, his sexuality, New Zealand, his miseries, his mind, that garage – I want to read Colin's book. So last Sunday I transcribed every word from my taped interview, printed it out, and faxed the 16 pages to Colin.

It took five hours to listen back to that interview. Five hours of listening to a dead man's voice.

I should have thought, *A year later, he went to Shoreditch to die.* But I wasn't searching for clues. I suppose it's a failure of the imagination. I didn't understand. I didn't see. All I thought of was there and then, a lunch in Wellington on a hot summer's day, when Justin Fashanu ate a bacon, lettuce and tomato sandwich, and said to the waitress, 'Can we have some tomato sauce, please? When you're ready. No rush.'

17 April 1999

ANDY

TWO SHORES. It pays to have rich friends, and I stayed Friday night on Waiheke Island, invited by chums who had rented a house above Palm Beach. That was nice. I went for a dip the next afternoon, built a city in the sand – moat, church, the Warehouse, sewerage pond – with some kids. Then I caught the 5pm ferry back to town, to board the 6pm train to Mt Maunganui for my brother Paul's 50th birthday. That was brilliant. Another brother, Mark, had driven over from Kawhia. We stayed up all night and walked to the beach at dawn; Paul could tell by the sound from his house that the surf was low, and he was right. We all agreed that the sand dunes looked sick, puny, worn out, not like the monsters covered with lupin when we were kids. Mark drove me back to Auckland on Sunday afternoon. My wife called my mobile phone as we approached Hamilton in pouring summer rain, and she said, 'Bill just phoned. Something terrible has happened.'

Third shore. Earlier that day, something like 1.30pm, in Golden Bay, Nelson, Andy drowned. He was in a kayak. It had flipped over. Those are some of the facts. But what Jenny said on the phone was, 'Andrew Heal's dead.'

And that's how it starts. Sitting in a clapped-out car, looking out the front window at thick, heavy rain, boring Hamilton minutes away, 10 to seven on a Sunday in January, a phone too small and pathetic to receive news as unbelievable as that.

He was the deputy editor of *Metro* magazine, he was 28, he was engaged to Cath, he was the son of Warwick and Kate, the brother of Greg, Fraser and Duncan, the friend of something like 300 people who sat in long rows at his funeral held in a school hall in Richmond on Thursday afternoon. The weather was beautiful, the nicest I've seen anywhere all this summer. I have no idea how everyone kept it together well enough to hold back from just howling.

He was 28, and that's the worst thing. He rocked, he was brilliant at his job, gentle, charming, fond of company and a drink, always happy to act the goat – he had a running gag about becoming the author of a book called *Famous Nelsonians* and its sequel, *Other Famous Nelsonians*; he liked to watch Mike Hosking on *Breakfast*. He was excellent at sports. At *Metro*, his run-up and bowl were devastating during office cricket, when we used a cardboard tube for a bat and a row of plastic skittles as the wickets. As a footballer, his passing was fluent; it was his astute lay-off that led me to deliver a fulminating left-foot screamer which sent the ball sailing over a dividing wall and into the *North & South* offices, landing, apparently, on the desk of poor old Warwick Roger, whose startled cry made Andrew laugh, and he had such a great laugh.

He was fun, and he could be intolerable to work with, one of those perfectionists you hear about but seldom meet; he was resolute. One of his brothers said at the funeral that he idolised Andy. Well, join the queue: I often saw how he inspired a kind of worship among other journalists, and he deserved that. It was always really easy to remark that he was the best magazine writer of his generation, because it was so obviously true.

'We were nine, and now we're eight,' Bill said, between gasps, and dropping his head and then raising it to dunk his snoot in a large gin, at his home that Sunday night. The eight remaining *Metro* staff were at their favourite bar, HQ, near the waterfront, the next afternoon; we sat inside, then outside, then inside, straying from tables and chairs, lost, quiet, hopeless. 'Come over tonight and we'll tell Andrew stories,' said Tim, and we sat in his flat, with Veronica and Jenny, dumb with grief.

All week at the *Listener* I wanted to whack someone. And then Thursday, the flight into Nelson, the hot day, the black suit, three heartbreaking hours at a funeral celebrating Andrew, telling Andrew stories, with Andrew – who grew up reading *Shoot!* magazine, where football managers routinely said of promising young players, 'The boy's a bit special' – in a coffin with an Arsenal scarf draped over it.

And it doesn't finish. Not for Cath, or his family, or his best friends, or workmates. He was someone people were proud of, and admired, respected, loved. 'I can't imagine a world without Andrew in it,' Tim said that Sunday night when he picked up the phone. Grief keeps him in it, and memory – 28 years of Andrew Heal, great guy, an Echo and the Bunnymen quiff as a teenager, 52 Bob Dylan CDs, skilled at rattling his desk with a pair of drumsticks, in love with Cath, amazed that his dad supported Charlton Athletic, a big fan of weddings, and with the 21st Century barely awake, popping into work on Saturday morning to leave Jenny a memo, then flying to Nelson, covered in a white sheet the next day. Final shore.

29 January 2000

GONE

INCREDIBLY ENOUGH, Andrew continues to be dead. I would have thought enough was enough after eight months. He died in January, in Nelson, in water. At his funeral, his father Warwick said he was told that Andrew was given CPR, but he was so bewildered that he thought, 'Why the hell are they giving Andrew the Consumer Price Index?'

But that was in January, in Nelson, and anywhere you go now Andrew remains dead. He was a friend of mine. We ended up working together at *Metro* magazine. He had a photo of Bob Dylan on his desk. We once hived off with my wife to Waiheke Island for the day, and mucked around, and missed the bus going back, so we hitched a lift to the ferry; back at his flat, I counted all his Bob Dylan CDs, about 50 of the things, and said, 'For fuck's sake! What are you playing at?'

I went drinking last Friday night at the Alhambra. When I got home, I went through my CD collection until I found a compilation album by Spirit, an American band from the 60s and 70s. I bought it last year because they did a really cool version of 'Like a Rolling Stone' by Bob Dylan. I remember saying to Andrew how much he'd love this performance, that it was the ultimate 'Like a Rolling Stone', loads better than Dylan's own recordings, but I never actually believed he would like it that much. I played the song last Friday night at a ridiculously loud volume, over and over again, thinking how cool it was, how dynamic and ringing and intense, how you couldn't hear most of the words because he whispered the lyrics, and how Andrew probably would not have approved because of that very fact, but I kept playing it, and thinking of Andrew, and I was so drunk and so frenzied that I hoped it was loud enough for him to hear.

Tom died two weeks ago, in Melbourne, and I suspect he will also insist on remaining dead. He was pretty much my closest friend when I lived in Wellington a long time ago. We were both gainfully unemployed, and would spend whole days at his flat while he made cups of tea, delivered brilliant, fuming speeches about literature – he had books in the hallway, in the laundry, in the sink – and played records. I flung a whole bunch of CDs around last Friday night in an attempt to find something that excited his imagination and met his standards of what was art. We had similar tastes. We loved the Fall, and the Velvet Underground, and Jonathan Richman, and Pere Ubu, but New Zealand music was also vitally important to us – we both loathed Chris Knox, and adored Bill Direen. And so after playing 'Like a Rolling Stone' about eight times I played *Modern Dance* by Pere Ubu, and 'Son of Cronos' and 'Grey Goose' by Bill Direen, but it was exhausting, hopeless, no use, because Tom is dead. For all his superb talk, there is no evidence to suggest he has anything more to say about that.

He was lively, emotional, constant. Sometimes we even got out of the house. On one visit, he dragged me into the sunshine for what he claimed would be a short trot. We ended up walking for bloody hours. It involved beating our way through some bush at the end of his street, where freshwater crayfish hid beneath rocks in a mountain stream, and then up into a vast hunk of private land. There were a few fences here and there, and the occasional sign which muttered something about how trespassers should keep out.

God knows what we talked about. All I remember about that is laughing my head off – Tom was in great spirits that day, with the sun on his pale South Island skin, passing over his packet of chocolate biscuits at judicious intervals. He had a cunning, wolfish smile, and a terrific capacity for hating all the right things. His humour was merciless. We became friends from the moment we met.

'How much further?' I kept bleating, just to make him laugh. It was a great day, two mates on an epic outing, young guys who were always anxious, worried, uncertain, looking at a wide, blue sky full of possibilities. The land finally fell away to a hillside. We slid down through thick bush, and found ourselves in a petrified forest. It was dark, almost black, and the stillness and the absolute quiet completely silenced us. The trees were tall, ancient, frozen, as pale as ghosts. At the bottom of the cliff, we stumbled onto a road, and there was the sea in front of us. We stood there blinking, and looked behind us at the forest, and probably said something profound like, 'Bloody hell. How about that?'

I tried to put the trees in my drunken, buzzing head last Friday night, with Bill Direen and Pere Ubu striking up a racket, but I flopped down on the couch and all I thought was, Tom is dead, apparently and probably forever.

9 September 2000

MANGROVIA

MY LIFE has become a David Attenborough nature programme since moving address to rent a house that overlooks a big, thick mangrove. I sit with my cat on the edge of our backyard and watch herons, and eels, and ducks, and two good shags, and the tide from a nearby bay shuffling in and then shuffling out along the creek, and we sometimes hoof down the hill to look at everything at close range. A strange kind of succulent, long-fingered, green and shameless red, covers the ground. Its soft sheet tucks itself in before the mangrove trees, which have a pale bark, almost silver when it glints in the sunlight.

We like to watch. The herons – there are three, sometimes four – like to roost in the tops of the same mangroves during the day. At about 7pm, as regular as commuters, they fly in a wide circle, then make their way to a stand of pine trees. They are quiet and superb in the air: the line from their neck to their chest has a very fine, dramatic scoop, and when they land, stretching their wings, they seem huge. But with their wings by their sides, they become wrapped up like small parcels.

Yes, and the eels assuming boneless Ss and sometimes surfing above the water, and the stone-faced mangroves as silent as 3am, and the absurd tootings and garglings and blatherings of so many different birds, and the fact that two weeks ago there were 12 ducklings, and now only eight – rats live on no evil star. And of course the mud. Footprints unglue its thin veneer and expose the pitch blackness of methane, hydrogen sulphide and zero oxygen. Absolutely nothing can live in such necessary filth. But – and this is where the Attenborough programme of my life these days turns to despair – a lot of stuff takes up residence anyway.

Litter. Bags of it. How many bags? On three missions so far, I have filled five big rubbish bags with chip packets, and straws, and bottles, and tampons, and sheets of plastic; the inventory also includes a child's badminton racquet and a hypodermic needle. Bloody diabetics. Beneath the mangroves, among its ring of pneumatophores which act as lungs, there is enough household refuse to fill a household.

It's a disgrace. And in the creek, there are tyres, and huge things made of iron, and . . . ah, but what have we here, placed along the banks of the creek? Brightly coloured signs placed by Metrowater. The fine print reads, 'Please assis in cleaning up our harbour by reporting any unusual discharges in the waterway.'

Well, you know me, always happy to assis. I called the advertised number: 624-2525. A woman answered. She said I had the wrong number. Great start. Telecom's directory assistance pointed me in the right direction, and I was put through to someone at Metrowater called Mike. It was 4pm on the Friday before Labour Weekend. No doubt the last thing Mike, as someone who works for one of the most reviled public companies in town, wanted to deal with that at that particular time was either a dissatisfied customer or churlish media. The poor devil got both.

I told him that a lot of litter appears after high rainfall floods the stormwater pipes leading into the creek. Mike found that 'unlikely'. I said it was so likely that it was a fact. Unimpressed, he claimed the city council's recently installed litter trap, which is about the size of a bathtub and floats in the creek, did a 'reasonable job'. I said it was fairly unreasonable that it had failed to trap enough junk to fill five rubbish bags.

In any case, he said, the city council were responsible for creek maintenance. I told him about the Metrowater signs. He found their existence 'highly unlikely'. Again, he didn't know what he was talking about. Well, I said, could he do anything about removing a bicycle that some shithead had recently dumped into the creek beneath a bridge. It would not fit into a rubbish bag, I said, and added that I regarded it as an 'unusual discharge'. He seemed to find that quite likely, and said he would place a few calls.

I await, as they say, with interest. At least I hadn't nagged Mike, as I planned, to provide me with gumboots and a pair of gloves for the next time I risk infections by picking up litter.

But there is also the small matter of pollutants and sewage which flow into the creek, and subsequently the harbour: it stinks to low hell, and doesn't look too good either. When the pipes flood, the rushing water is brown, bilious, downright libellous. Mike said Metrowater was currently researching more effective pipeflow systems.

That would be nice. I like mangroves. I want them to be happy. It occurs to me that perhaps I should make someone's life hell as I work towards this small, good thing.

6 November 1999

THE PEARL

THE MORNING streets of Bluff are as still as the vases on every windowsill, as the craypots rusting at the back of vast barns, as the seagull lying dead and spotlessly white on its back in an empty section. An unpainted buoy with a slot hacked through it acts as a letterbox. Someone plays loud rock music in a house up on the foothills; next door, an old man with a thin mouth sits on his porch, and looks out to sea. There is dyslexic graffiti on the side of a shed – 'MARLEY RLUES'. A sack of coal is taped to paper over a smashed window. Smoke rises then slumps out of chimneys; there is nothing quite like the peculiar sadness of the smell of coal fires on summer mornings.

A quiet (pop. 2,500), lovely, deserted town at the very end of New Zealand, but the facts are completely different seconds after the stroke of midday at the Bluff Bakery. The place is packed. You can't hear yourself think for the wild laughter of old ladies sipping on their tea. A young guy with a proper Mohican mohawk says, 'Two fingers, please,' pointing at long sweet things on the counter. The lamingtons are delicious. You might have to tramp to Reefton for a cheaper bag of hot chips.

Next door at the taxi company, Marie has bought four crumbed chicken drumsticks, and is feeding the bones to her two pups on the carpet. You used to, she says, get maybe a dozen free feeds during the season – she means an oysterman's catch, the oysters fresh from the bags dredged from their beds in Foveaux Strait. 'The best oysters.' But since the fishing quotas, and since the bonamia virus destroyed an estimated 700 million oysters, you'd be lucky now to get two or three feeds.

A used-to-be-town – there are no banks, no chemist shops; the Ocean View freezing works has closed. About 24 oyster boats would go out fishing. Now there are 14. 'You've got to wait for someone to die before you get a job on these boats,' says Rex Ryan, a skipper who has a crew of five.

The commercial season is over, but Ryan has won the tender to dredge up to a million oysters until next month, as part of an enhancement programme. Spawning oysters are put aside for research; the rest are sold by local firm Barnes exclusively to Woolworths Big Fresh, whose PR company Palace Plus paid for my trip, and performed good deeds in Invercargill and Bluff by spreading around some of that nice Auckland money.

All taxi drivers and waitresses were given generous tips. A dreadful piece of news in the *Southland Times* also led to PR largesse: it was about an Invercargill woman whose flatmates skipped town, leaving her with a $539 overdue power bill to Contact Energy, who cut her off ('heartless and irresponsible,' wrote David Melmoth in the newspaper's letters page), forcing her and her four children to live by candlelight since 19 October. I donated $50 towards the bill at the *Times* front office, and hope it helps. Any quibbling by Palace Plus when presented with the receipt will be reported.

Woolworths is charging about $17.95 for a dozen Bluff oysters. As for the precious leftover spawn, they are in the hands of Jake Keogh, a marine scientist from Otago University, who is conducting trials to resettle the oysters in Foveaux Strait. Tall, wild haired, Irish, he works from a large shed in Bluff during the enhancement season. Water splashed into a gash on the side of his sandshoe. 'These,' he says, peering at specks inside a 5,000-litre tank, 'are the business.' There were 10 million of these half-a-millimetre specks of larvae in his care, taken from the Barnes factory each morning. 'The oysters are taken from the boat and put in a coolstore overnight,' he explained, and was then seized by an uncontrollable mirth, stabbing at the air: 'At 7.30am, it's cold steel for everybody. Hoi! Ha! Yah!'

Afterwards, in the smoko room overlooking Bluff wharf, he became very sober. 'This represents the first sustained and serious attempt to restore the oyster beds.' Is it working? 'A month ago, we effectively began a three-month programme, and our aim at the end of that is to have some unequivocal answers to that particular question . . . I'm optimistic.'

Get on with, it grumble some oystermen, who believe that the special fishing permit is ruining the spawning season and masquerades as a money-making enterprise. 'It's not a way of life any more,' says Rex Ryan. 'It's a business.'

His boat came in past Land's End, past the Tiwai smelter, past banks of lupin, past the Bluff pubs (Flynn's, the Eagle, the Golden Age), and tied up at the wharf. He is one of 25 Ryans in the Bluff directory; his family go back to the days of whaling. Ex-army – he served in Vietnam – he doesn't drink or smoke, and up until last year ran up Bluff Hill every morning. He went out to the Straits at 4am, and has returned with 30 sacks. 'Go on,' he said, and put the cold steel to half a dozen shells. It was strange to be at the source of the most famous food in New Zealand. They tasted the best, the very best.

20 November 1999

FAIRLIE

HOW STRANGE and how weightless it is to return to Auckland after only a few days in Fairlie – a small town (pop. 600) in the Mackenzie Country, near Timaru, and Pleasant Point, and Kimbell, and Dead Horse Stream. I left nothing behind but footprints in the frost. The days were blue and clear, not a shred of wind, and after cold, still nights, the big dark sky scribbled with stars, the mornings were white. Under the bridge and at the Opihi River, which runs alongside the town, the water was so shocked by the low temperatures that it steamed, like when you open the door of the fridge freezer. You could drown out the sound of birds by walking on the grass – the sods of earth crack under your feet. There were a few fat sheep in front yards, as motionless as rocks. Above everything, the Two Thumbs Range, covered in snow, stared down on the town, the river, the sheep, the footprints.

You should go there at once. What a lovely place. It even has shops. Most rural towns in New Zealand with faintly absurd names make a virtue of that fact – Foxton, Bulls, Blackball – and Fairlie sells nice jams and an assortment of crafts at Fairlie Interesting. The local gymnasium, inevitably, is Fairlie Fit, and the local bakery is much better than its modest shopsign, Fairlie Good Bakery.

There are also two pubs, a motel, a bloody good restaurant in the old library, and a tearoom that deserves to win national awards. Outside the newsagent, there is a board which reads, NEWSPAPERS. MAGAZINES. BOOKS. LINGERIE. ('A copy of the *High Country Herald*, please, and a pair of panties.') And on Riddle Street, a second-hand clothes store advised its hours of business in a sign on the

77

window: 'Monday, closed. Tuesday, closed. Wednesday, closed. Thursday, closed. Friday, open 10am–12.00pm'.

As well, there is a handsome retirement home, formerly the maternity hospital, which is conveniently or cruelly just down the road from the town cemetery. It's nice walking among the gravestones, and the tall trees, and the dead, and a memory of the dead. Probably the saddest inscription I've ever read is in that plot. It marks a soldier killed in 1916. It reads:

When he left us with his comrades
He nobly went to take his chance.
Now he's sleeping in a soldier's grave
On the battlefields of France.

You should at least stop while passing through. Tour coaches make a point of it, spilling out grateful Japanese to the public toilets. Over summer a few years ago, an enterprising local set up business in the reserve right beside the toilets, where he sat in a deck chair waiting for tourists to watch him shear a pen of sheep he carted in on a trailer. He had a sign that read, SHEAR ENTERTAINMENT. Apparently the local council have refused to give him a permit. Instead, in an effort to drum up passing trade, they have spent $800,000 on upgrading the main street look. There are flower beds, and rest tables, and seats, and paving stones. It looks Fairlie attractive.

For a more active pastime, there is an iceskating rink next to the caravan park. Perhaps it will freeze over this winter. Already, though, it is exquisite – a large, black rectangle of water beneath bare trees, and floodlights, and it also has a pavilion. Inside, there are colour photographs of people skating at night.

But all I wanted to do was walk around, beneath the larches

and the poplars, my arms folded in a sheepskin jacket against the cold of morning and the cold of night, and then wander back to my father's house. He had a photo I'd never seen before of a man cobbling a shoe. I asked, 'Who's that old geezer?' and he said it was his grandfather, Leopold; it had been taken maybe 50 or 60 years ago, in Innsbruck. The guy is as far back as we know of anyone with our surname, although a relative in Austria reckons there is a cemetery in Crete full of dead blokes called Braunias, dating 1,000 years before Christ. My brother Mark has just passed through the islands of Samos, Santorini, Ios and Naxos, and sent Dad a postcard. 'Everyone here has recognised the Greek in Braunias – one asking me if I spoke Greek, or did my father. They say the name is peculiar to the islands – not a common name, but also not unusual. It seems to originate from western Crete . . . Anyway, that confirms the suspicion.'

Hmm. I have never been remotely interested in family history, but I liked the sound of all that – the vague, obscure travels of 3,000 years for a Braunias to leave Crete and arrive in Fairlie, where you pass by two men on the main street discussing winter feed, and a woman saying to her friend, 'Thanks for keeping me up with the latest scandal!'; and you notice that telephone wires hit by sunlight become streaks of white light, and a sheep truck driving along a shingle road sends up a cloud of dust that looks like fog; and you look behind you, and see your footprints in the frost.

10 June 2000

HOT WATER SAILOR

VERY NEARLY my favourite short story is 'The Swimmer', by American writer John Cheever. It hares off on a single terrific idea: the main character, Neddy Merrill, is relaxing beside a swimming pool owned by friends when he realises something momentous. 'His own house stood eight miles to the south . . . it occurred to him that he could reach his home by water.' He maps it out, charts his course. There are exactly 14 other swimming pools, as well as one public pool, which he can dive into and paddle home: 'He seemed to see, with a cartographer's eye, that string of swimming pools, that quasi-subterranean stream that curved across the county.'

You could do that in New Zealand. You could chart a stream, braided by lawns and streets, that curves across the land – you could follow a line of hot pools and thermal springs. We're talking a hell of a lot more distance than eight miles, but we're also talking a hell of a lot more comfort once you arrive at each new soak. A typically fulsome article in *New Zealand Geographic* (October 1998) maps out 107 hot springs, from Lake Omapere in the Far North, to Henry Burn in Fiordland. Go west, to Arawhata, near New Plymouth; go east, to Morere, near Hastings; and hoof offshore, to Great Barrier Island, Whale Island and White Island.

Is there one explorer who has navigated their way to the whole wet, steaming lot? Which wrinkled soul holds the record? Have there been new and secret discoveries where magma has boiled the jug and sent up all that delicious heat to an obscure hole in the ground? And does New Zealand get more New Zealand than the simple-minded pleasure of dipping your ass into a hot spring?

Everyone who scoots off to a hot pool – and there can be few of us, rich or poor, mad or boring, sick or gymnastic, who have never visited these sensational puddles – returns to brag. You hear them go on about the unspoiled pools at Tokaanu and Ngawha, the fun they had at Maruia, the feel of the night air cooling their face as they float down Mt Te Aroha after a good, long soak in a private tub. Fair enough. Good luck to them. As such, I can boast that I recently visited hot pools in both islands in the same week.

On the Monday night, I lowered myself into the Palm Springs hot pools in Parakai, near Helensville, about 30 minutes out of Auckland. This is such a brilliant place. They do a bloody good toasted sandwich. You can smoke in peace, and take your cold beer or your pot of tea out to the pool. There is a friendly dog and an even more friendly cat: there is peeling paint, and a sign saying someone called Captain Cash once killed his wife on the premises: an old bloke goes there every day and talks to you about his kumaras. The more excitable go across the road to a hot pool that has slides. None of that nonsense at Palm Springs, which has a soft, quiet, exquisite kind of gentleness about it, and is probably very good for your bunions.

Three days later, I got very excitable at Hanmer Springs, north of Christchurch. You have of course heard of Hanmer Springs. It has to be the most famous hot pool in New Zealand. It's also become a swept-up and very commercial operation, with sauna and steam suites, and therapeutic massage rooms – my pampered wife spent an hour up to her pretty ears in creamy, fizzing mud, and emerged docile, shiny as a new coin and most pleased with the lightness of her being. Meanwhile, I shot down a pitch-black waterslide and felt perhaps as close as I've ever come to death. Most definitely I felt I had made a dreadful mistake. Talk about blind panic. The thing seems endless. You travel at incredible speeds. It twists left, it twists right, it twists the straightest of minds. It threw me from side to side like a peanut trapped in a cocktail shaker; witnesses remarked on the awful clattering I made as I bounced off the walls on my terrible descent. In short, it was tremendous fun, and too right I went unsteadily back for more.

As well, there are seven open-air thermal pools, some in the shape of streams nestled among rocks, and three sulphur pools stoked by the very fires of hell. A lot of water, a lot of people – dramatic Japanese in pink bikinis, hobbling coots, the fat and the painfully thin who clatter down waterslides. Couples canoodled in what a friend leeringly refers to as 'cuddle puddles'. And although there was much whooping to be heard, the atmosphere was restful, admirably content, as all that flesh dozed in all that vaporous goodness.

Cheever's story 'The Swimmer' ends in tragedy. No such unhappiness when you voyage the string of hot pools curving across New Zealand. The steam and the minerals subtract any kind of soreness in your bones; all seems well with the world, as you – I love the way this sounds – take the waters.

14 October 2000

COASTER

SEASALT, HONEYSUCKLE, lupins, grapefruit, feijoas, radishes, Rotorua sulphur, Coromandel green, Indian curry – New Zealand smells great. You really can follow your nose. A thousand or maybe a million different scents invade the air on either coast and rise up from the land; even the dullest of snoots are filled with aromas, tangs and various whiffs. But the very greatest smell, the most pleasing and obvious and national, is coal in Greymouth.

Go there and honk it up at once. Nothing beats it. Honestly. Once smelt, never forgotten – its warm, black pungency has a kind of thrilling malevolence about it. Hacked out from under the ground, it has a smell which simmers with rage. Well-meaning bores drone on about the healing powers of crystals. The smell of coal has a definite energy which goes back to some distant, buried past - a primal smell, a medieval smell, a colonial smell. And it smells best of all in Greymouth, and the exact place is by the river, near the Railway Hotel, on the railway tracks, where the coal just sits there, raw and hard, reeking up a storm, in an open wagon.

Only a mad bastard would romanticise the actual labour of coal mining. Mervyn Thompson once wrote a play about it. But the smell of coal in Greymouth has its own romance, its own beauty. It hit me like a ton of . . . coal, one late winter's afternoon on a quiet Sunday in my own distant past, when I first arrived as a Wellington fish out of water starting a new job in a new town. And there it was again, when I recently swanned in as a day-tripper on the TranzAlpine train from Christchurch, which drops you off by the river, near the Railway Hotel.

It is not fresh or startling news to say that this is one of the great train journeys of the world. It's a classic ride, four hours and 25 minutes of snow and lakes and beech, from coast to coast. What excited me most, though, was when the train hooked up to the line alongside the Grey River: next stop, Greymouth. The high riverbank cliffs give way suddenly, and there's the flat town, slinking towards the treacherous bar and the white, foaming Tasman Sea.

The return journey sets off an hour later. Stay. Not just for the smell of coal, which for some reason is strongest at dusk, its dark scent at home in the dark light. Greymouth is well worth a good, long gawk. It feels like the most forgotten town in New Zealand. There are other places more far flung, isolated, amputated. None exists with such independence or strength of character.

It used to suffer terrible floods – when I lived there, the water poured over the sandbags, and was knee-deep in my local bar one night when a bloke canoed through the front doors and asked the bartender for a bottle of stout. The mayor back then, Barry Dallas, who would attend council meetings with his dog Morgan at his side, talked about moving the town. The shock tactic helped mobilise the building of the town's flood wall along Mawhera Quay. You can now sit on top of it on chairs and watch the sunlight burn the surface of the Grey River as it passes safely out to sea.

In the town itself, attractions include the ABC Quick Lunch Cafe, which at this time of year serves succulent whitebait sandwiches on white bread for $5.50. The only printing press in New Zealand that is visible from the street whizzes out copies of the *Greymouth Evening Star* behind glass. Second-hand bookstore Clocktower Collectables, run by legendary pressman Pat Taylor, stocks a first-rate New Zealand section – Graham Billing's 1969 spy novel set in Wellington, *The Alpha Trip*, with a lurid jacket design by Barbara Walton, fetched only $3 ('The Man with the Golden Soufflé', page 53).

There are bargains everywhere you look on the West Coast. The government bought off its logging industry for $92 million . . . Unable to touch its timber and control its own destiny, it sits on the money, $23 million deposited in banks in Greymouth, Westport, Reefton and Hokitika for the next three months, until a trust board is elected. In the meantime, six marinated pork steaks sell for $10 at Westmeat butchers in Greymouth, and $78,000 buys a house with original high-timbered ceilings and a built-in rimu bookcase in Ross.

The forgotten coast – except during the whitebait season, which is lousy at the moment, and in March, when Hokitika hosts its famous Wild Foods Festival. Actually, Hokitika is a brilliant place any time of the year, with its elegant clocktower, its comfortable cinema, its eels as big as serpents in Waterworld, its museum boasting a 45,000-piece Meccano construction of the old Grey River gold dredge, and its historic Southland Hotel run by the O'Connor family since 1885. Upstairs, in the hotel's Tasman View restaurant, you can chow down and gape at the long beach scribbled with driftwood and the sun setting on the long sea.

Late that night, from my bedroom window, I saw red sparks flying out to sea. A huddle of teenagers were whooping it up on the sand beside a roaring fire; two girls ran into the cold tide, their shrieks unheard and unnoticed on this separate coast.

21 October 2000

MANGROVIA

THERE IS A photo I like. There is a heron in it. Intent and grey as a pencil smudge, the bird stands on a mangrove branch. And there is black, shimmering water, and mangroves as healthy as a horse, and silence – I don't know if I'll ever be able to move away from the creek which runs at the back of my rented house in downtown Auckland. It's taken hold. It shuts the rest of this stupid city's trap. It sits in its room all day and all night. It couldn't care less if I lived or died. It looks fantastic; it looks ugly as sin. It puts up with all sorts of nonsense. It can barely breathe, but it has things like herons in it.

And it also has things like shit in it. Raw sewage overflows into the creek an estimated 160 times a year. One test has measured a level of 480,000 faecal coliforms per 100 litres of water; the accepted bathing level is 200. Another test claimed 1.6 million enterococci – a member of that charming family, faecal streptococci – per 100 litres, when the standard New Zealand level flashes a red light once it exceeds 136.

The statistics are courtesy of a residents' pressure group that formed in 1989. These people are saints. I have their gospels inside two whopping ringbinders, lent to me by one of the loudest and busiest group activists, Nicola Legat, the deputy editor of *Metro* magazine. The paperwork includes all their official transactions with various council bodies. My favourite is the 1990 document which deals with the council engineer's idiotic solution to a sick creek: concrete it. You expect the next paragraph to suggest that the ozone layer be fixed by stretching a bloody big tarpaulin over Earth.

The group successfully lobbied against turning the creek into a drain, and their constant nagging has helped influence the council to separate the main stormwater and sewage pipe by next year – civic leaders had wanted to delay the operation by 30 years. The work means that overflows will cease, but not entirely: council will wait about 10 years to separate two other pipes. 'The fact of their existence had never been raised,' notes Legat, and by this stage in my reading I wanted to stick those pipes right up council's ass.

Well, such battles with that dreariest of fields – local body politics – are played out all over New Zealand. And that's always been my point in writing about the creek that I muck around in for hours and hours, either just looking, thanks, or cleaning up litter: it could be anywhere. This is my fifth 'Mangrovia' column over the past year or so ('All you write about is mangroves and tearooms!' some once-famous ninny screeched at me recently), but I've never mentioned the actual name of the creek. Who cares what it's called? It could be any New Zealand waterway polluted by sewage and disgusting amounts of litter. It could well describe a creek or a river or a beach near you.

A number of readers have written in saying that they, too, patrol their local creek, river, etc, to collect rubbish. Matt from Nelson radio station Planet called to discuss his own efforts to clean up a nearby beach. 'Why do people dump stuff in places like this?' he asked. Showing the kind of quick wit and intellect which has made me such an attractive asset in the modern media, I said, 'I dunno.' But I do know that some people try to do something to make this country a bit more like it looks in those nice postcards we produce.

Legat's ringbinder opens with her scribbled note above a form letter sent out by the Department of Conservation in 1989: 'How it all began!' Her group had been alerted to the fact it was Conservation Week. They were inspired to plant trees by the creek. They kept going. They got political, demanded change, attended undoubtedly boring meetings, got stuff done. You read it here first, probably because no one else will bother publishing the information, but this year's Conservation Week kicks off on 9 August. There you go. Just a subtle hint.

All I do is wander around by myself with rubbish bags, and pick up garbage, and have managed to persuade a top bloke called Mike at the city council to send teams of workers to make raids on some of the worst eyesores in the creek, which is beginning to look . . .

I ducked into the mangroves on Saturday, to where the creek turns away from the public boardwalk and is hidden from view. A runaway dog called Jake followed me in; he ran around while I filled up two rubbish bags, until I came to a side-creek which was too deep to cross. The tide was running out. I sat down on a mangrove trunk and watched the water flow, fast and clear and spilling, and it really was a lovely sight, almost heartbreaking, and Jake sat beside me, and a heron flew overhead, and it rasped, 'Gaaah!' I love that stupid bird.

22 July 2000

MILK, NO SUGAR

AND SO THIS column's search for good, decent New Zealand tearooms – the kind of establishment which pours coffee straight from the pot, and serves you an egg sandwich dropped straight from the chook – continues with news of a vast reward. A few weeks ago I asked readers to write in and name their favourite coffee lounge. It was my third attempt at whipping up frenzy on the subject this year; as a sweetener, I announced the best, most touching letter would win $20 from my own pocket.

My warmest congratulations, then, to Cushla of Dunedin. Her vote is for **Governor's Coffee Shop**. In her own words: 'For the nostalgic nosher this is a taste of NZ as she used to be. Start your day the old-fashioned way with bacon and eggs, or the house special – sossies, hash browns, tomato, eggs and toast. For the delicate constitution, perhaps pancakes (no crepes around here, mate!) or just toast with lashings of butter.'

Trained medical staff had to revive me at this point. I had died and gone to buttered heaven. But Cushla went on, relentless, wanton, hungry: 'Muesli with fruit and yoghurt if you must, but don't forget the obligatory coffee, served in a mug . . . How about a light lunch? Try a toasted sandwich oozing cheese (that aromatic golden brown you get when you massage butter over the outside before putting it under the grill), with or without onions, mushrooms, pineapple, tomato . . .

'On a winter noon may I recommend their thick and satisfying soup, and garlic bread with creamy butter nestled in its inviting grooves. Maybe you fancy baked beans or spaghetti on toast, or a nice meat pie . . . Nachos and a moist mound of sour cream . . . Ham and lettuce sandwich . . . Solid scones and muffins . . . Banana splits . . . Chocolate, apple or carrot cake . . . A mug of hot, steaming chocolate . . . '

Bloody hell. Governors is the guv'nor, no doubt about it; as for Cushla, I have to be frank and say that I love her. Round eyed and drooling at her way with a menu, I would be flattered ('You'll have to come down here . . . I think we're on first-name terms after this intimate encounter, don't you?', she added) to put my feet under her table. My shout.

Thanks to everyone who responded. Ngaire of Te Puke wrote to praise the **Mayfair** in her home town, and also the **Copper Kettle** in Ngatea and **Ronnie's Cafe** in Matamata: 'The truck drivers eat here.' Jackie of St Heliers gave specific directions to the **Brown Owl** – 'Going south on Highway 27, it is on the left as you come into the township' – but I couldn't read her handwriting when she came to the crucial spelling of the actual town. And so somewhere south on Highway 27 there are 'delicious home-made sandwiches, clean toilets and a donkey or two in the paddock out the back'.

Someone with an illegible signature in Fendalton recommended **Perry's**, opposite the Christchurch Polytechnic. Dorothy of Whangarei was effusive about her local tearoom, **Bliss**, and an unnamed cafe in Waipu ('It is on the left side of The Centre, as you head south, and opposite the cenotaph') and the **Alpine** in Taupo. By email, Elizabeth raved about the **21st Century Cafe** in Wellesley Street West, Auckland, and also the **Pioneer** in Willis Street, Wellington. Allow me to declare a fondness that stretches over 10 years and confirm that the Pioneer is one of the greatest coffee lounges in the entire country.

Several other correspondents tweaked the rules. Patricia of

Napier wished to rave about the **Red Tulip** cakeshop in Palmerston North: 'Outside there are even those little cubes of thickened glass, set in the footpath, set in time.' Chris of Upper Hutt is a fiend for a nice hot cup of tea, and on that prejudice – how he went on about 'the flavour of tea is spoiled by light'; he even claimed he carries his own teabags everywhere he goes, 'as security' – voted for **Victuals** in Bulls, **Sea Breezes** in Picton, **Original Bakery** in Stoke and **Coppers** in Marton. Good man.

Mark of Gisborne, meanwhile, posted a fluent, compelling letter which traced the recent evolution of espresso slophouses in Gisborne. It was an invaluable document of decay and rot ('We're very much at the espresso end of the food chain these days') in that pleasant town, and reminded me that I have no business in ever visiting.

Last, and very much least, a howling bore by the name of N. Kolsen emailed to sneer at my entire attempt to celebrate good, decent coffee lounges. 'Cafe foods originated in Europe. Do yourself a favour, and educate yourself in these foods, educate others, and leave the snacks your mother made you at home.' Do yourself a favour, pal. Don't show your face around here. Fuck off. You make me sick to my otherwise quite contented stomach.

4 September 1999

I HATE YOU DEEPLY

HOPE YOU like the headline. It's a straight steal from a story by Daniel Clowes in issue two of his comic *Eightball*, which is the best thing I've read in the past 10 years. You should buy it. Back copies are available at selected comic stores, or you can contact his publisher, Fantagraphics, on 1-800-657-1100, in Seattle.

Clowes' 'I Hate You Deeply' litany includes 'people with personality, magnetism, and charisma, idealists, musclemen, watered-down nostalgia hounds, lowest common denominators, guys with short hair on top and long hair in back, anyone involved in insurance, medicine, law, or real estate, actors, models or anyone who places disproportionate importance on that kind of glorified service job, fashion plates, fanatics, Richard Simmons and his ilk, urban attention seekers . . . ' and more.

A work of art. Love his work, deeply. As such, all I can do is buy his comic, promote his genius and, as someone who knows no shame, rip him off.

I'm not the kind of fellow who hates easily. Just quickly, and horribly. Saturday is a good day for hate. This is usually when I step out with my lovely wife and treat her to a cooked breakfast. It's amazing how much fury a man can work up on his way to an innocent omelette.

Pavement hogs. What incredible rudeness. You know who I mean. The kind of couples, or sometimes three stupid friends, who waddle across the entire length of the sidewalk, their hips swaying lazily in the breeze, their progress slow and fat, making it impossible to pass – what utter bastards.

Teenagers. Ugh.

Old friends who you so desperately want to avoid that you hide inside butcher shops or pretend that all of a sudden you have an urgent errand in the other direction. Why don't they just stay home, *all the time*?

Cafe owners who charge an arm and a leg for a knuckle of food. Plus they always add such foulnesses as pesto, aioli, mayonnaise, etc, and *expect you to like it*. They don't deserve to live.

People with the right haircut and the correct shoes sitting outside cafes happily eating pesto, aioli, mayonnaise, etc. I suspect that some day they will all die.

Mondays to Fridays are possibly even more lethal. I get too wrapped up in my trade, its shorthand judgements, its continual gawping upon the activities of others, its demands on always having to write something; hatred becomes an occupational hazard.

Opinion columnists. They're all dismal. Apart from Joe Bennett, who is funny, and poised, and inviting; he thoroughly deserved to win the 1998 Qantas Award for best columnist, but that meant he claimed the title I had won the previous year, and so I hate him.

All stand-up comedians, most new New Zealand novelists, white rappers, short-film makers, exhibition curators, anyone involved in theatresports. I have a mean, small-minded theory that the pursuit of art in the late 20th century has led to a mass outbreak of self-delusion.

Critics. Really, where do they get off?

Muriel Newman, Roger Estall, Bill Birch, Kevin Roberts, anyone who belongs to the Liberterianz. But this is only because I'm a typical sandal-wearing, timidly left-leaning liberal who has no concrete alternatives to the way society is run.

Steve Braunias. Too often, I can't stand the sight of him – his duplicities, his shamelessness, his smoking, his face. From the 1938 classic *Enemies of Promise*, essayist Cyril Connolly writes: 'I have always disliked myself at any given moment; the total of such moments is my life.'

Yes, you can't go past a good dose of self-loathing. Actually, you can; novelist Graham Greene was miserable most of his life, but he kept his spirits up by playing a tremendous game called 'Hating People'. Happy or depressed, there are targets that await your scorn and contempt.

Trouts working in PR, marketing and human resources. Such jobs are total inventions which are of no use to anyone.

Idiots elevated to positions of importance, otherwise known as Duds With Jobs.

Go-getters, positive thinkers, motivational speakers, role models. They're running this country into the ground. At least I think they are. What do I know? I'm probably just jealous. It's not as if I've ever done anything impressive, or deserving of fame or huge financial reward.

Decisive people. God, what a drag they are.

Exhausting. Please, send in your own lists. We'll share our basic rages, our complex distempers. Write to 'Hating Steve' at the *Listener* address; a valuable archive will be created, and published at a later date. You owe it to your sense of justice. You owe it to New Zealand.

15 May 1999

HATE MAIL

YOU BET I welcome readers' letters, even the ones which are a variation of, 'Why doesn't Steve Braunias go fuck himself?' They are easy to spot in advance: the editor's PA bears down on my office with a jauntier than usual step, and her smile is quite openly malicious as she hands over the latest humourless condemnation. Admittedly, my first reaction is to cry like a baby. But it's nice to know that so many people feel so much rage. They care; they want change. Such themes were most definitely played out in the correspondence I recently invited on the subject of hate.

A few columns ago, I listed a number of things or people worthy of my contempt, and asked readers to send in their own lists. The response was heartening. New Zealand is full of good, admirable hate.

There is a hate which serves no purpose at all. It wears the stupid, sickening face of a bigot, a boor, a bitter wretch. But there was another character of hate that I heard about. It was indignant, and bewildered; it spluttered, 'How dare you!'; simply, it was outraged.

It was felt in the home, including the retirement home. 'I hate people who assume that if you are old, you are senile,' seethed a Waikane woman who signed herself as J. 'They call us "dear" in shops, little realising the savage thoughts behind those "sweet" old faces.' She went further: 'I hate those who say old people want to hear "Remembrance" and "Jesus Loves Me". One of these days, some ancient old lover of music will rise up and bite them.'

It was gender specific. 'I hate baby-boomer females who

scrutinise other women, po-faced, from shoes to throat, before committing to the face,' observed Patricia of Napier. And: 'Higher-mileaged women who wear draggy, monocoloured tracksuits, all sag, topped off with a knob of frizz.' Clearly, she had issues. But the big picture did not escape her firm eye: 'Frauds and shams who occupy positions of high power within the church, military or government.'

Someone with an illegible signature from Dargaville filled four pages with their anger. An edited highlight: 'I hate Christmas computer printouts. You know the ones that boast about little Chelsea's amazing exam results and flaunt the writer's wealth. "We drove through Germany before returning to NZ via Hawaii", knowing that all I've done is walked to the local shops.'

The correspondence was often personal – those hated included Barry Crump, 'Whassisname Delamare', Paul Holmes, Celine Dion, 'Sons who swear at you', Saatchi bore Kevin Roberts, 'Fathers who never take their daughters to Saturday netball', and Amway agents. All worthy objects of derision, but rather predictable; similarly, there were expected issues which inspired disgust, such as 'corporate fascism', the Bill of Rights, New Age health quackery, establishment health quackery, 'right-wing ideologues', telephone marketing, the millennium and jogging.

Yes. But hatred also calls for an individual voice, a finely tuned and original mind filled with various scorns, exasperations and unreasonable furies. Warren came to the party. The man is a prince of pique, a monarch of malice; his almighty peevishness spilled over a range of subjects, including garnish, live jazz, rugby, noise control officers, old people (sorry, J. of Waikanae!) and protesters.

Worryingly, his email disclosed the information that he had attended Mt Maunganui College and was a fool for soccer. Snap. I began to wonder whether I was writing to myself under an assumed name. But he also claimed he was national manager for a government department. Besides, there was no way I could compete with his spite.

He hated airtowels: 'Totally useless. I'm convinced they make your hands seem more damp after using them.' He hated loud, raucous groups of people at intimate restaurants: 'Naturally when I'm part of a loud, raucous group, I am the loudest and most obnoxious, because I know that those couples sitting in tables have all been loud and raucous in their time and all I'm doing is getting my own back.' He hated Good Kiwi Blokes: 'The ones that can take a bit of 4 x 2, a couple of rusty nails and an empty baked bean can and build an emergency weather balloon out of it when required. I hate that. They are all called Steve and they can fix anything. I'm always a nervous wreck when Steve the sparky comes around to fix something in our house. "Oh," he'll say, "It's just the multiple charge relays in the dampener that need realigning. No worries." Wankers!'

A good man, and a proud New Zealander. My sincerest thanks to everyone who replied – yes, you too, Carolyn of Owaka, South Otago, who concluded her superb foam-flecked ravings with, 'I hate people who disturb your image of yourself as a calm, settled person, and invite you to list your rages. Absolutely.'

26 June 1999

LOVE

INVITING READERS of the *Listener* to write in with their lists of things they most hate and despise – it later ran to two more columns – was good, harmless fun, even though it inevitably led to friends and strangers inquiring about my state of emotional health. But I'm as full of love as the next person consumed with numerous and assorted hatreds. I love on tap, without being asked, indiscriminately and often unwisely – my black, black heart is red with love. You could very easily say that most of this book is about things I love. Reviewers are welcome to do so.

Second-hand bookstores, mangroves, tearooms, Te Aroha, Greymouth, Fairlie, autumn, hot pools, the cold dead – they are all in here, all present and correct. And so is my wife, my family, a few of my friends. Reviewers might comment that most of the book is about myself. Bastards. Being me is the last place I look for something lovable. The first place is whatever is in front of my snoot.

Cats on the windowsill. Is there anything more picturesque? They sit there behind glass, staring out, safe and warm and smug, too cool to pull faces, while the bedlam of the world passes before their beautiful eyes. All cats go to heaven when they die, and they look at Jesus walking past the front yard as they sit on windowsills.

Salami in the fridge. A friend tells me that salami has the same addictive properties as chocolate. This is probably a nonsense – I have no great cravings for a salami cake – but it's true that salami is a rich and ingenious thing, with its paper wrapper and its discs of goodness. There should be free salami in schools.

Peter Frampton on the radio. From a building site during the day, or in a car late at night on the motorway, or anywhere you care to mention, 13 minutes and 42 seconds of the great man reinventing electricity on 'Do You Feel Like We Do' is an eternal and recommended madness.

Mail from the Bonus Bonds in the letterbox. It could be the monthly first prize of $300,000, and for a golden, shimmering moment you can see the shape of the Mediterranean, New York, Paris, all the wonders of the world, maybe even a new pair of shoes.

Perhaps these are all selfish. It's always better to share with those you love.

Will. My godson, and a top little six-year-old bloke. No doubt he has said the darndest things, but the first image of him that comes to mind is taking him on the bus to Auckland's waterfront on a day in summer, and sitting together on some steps by the wharf and eating iceblocks in happy, slurping silence.

Ivan. My oldest friend. Every time we see each other we end up sitting outside somewhere in the sun and drinking beer, and he always says the same sincere thing: 'This is the life.'

Tim. My most optimistic friend. Every time I bowl around to his place and get drunk and end up vomiting in his garden, he cheerfully crows the same thing: 'That's the way!'

George. My cat. He looks so cool sitting on the windowsill.

All great guys, but you can't beat the love of a good woman. Misogyny must be about the stupidest thing in the world. Even complete and utter bitches are born with the best chromosome. I've been in love three or four times, and it's better than winning Bonus Bonds. Possibly.

Palmerston North. 'Blimey,' I said. 'What the hell's that, and what's it doing there?' She said it was a birthmark. What deliciousness.

Padangbai. Walking along together as happy as clams in this shabby, charming fishing village in Bali, she said, 'Here. Put some suntan lotion on your snoot.' What genius to come up with a word like that. It burst in my head like a luscious, intoxicating fruit, and changed the way I thought about language for ever.

Outside a bottle store on a summer's day. While she waited in the carpark, I got some booze, and then walked back outside to see her standing against the iron railing with her arms outstretched, one leg raised, her face turned to the breeze, and the sunlight like fire on her hair. What langorousness. I asked for a kiss, and she said, 'Yes, please.'

A back garden at night. There were family, and friends, and lights strung up in the trees, and 'Girlie' by The Peddlers on cassette, and the bride wore white, and there were flowers in her hair, and to a question put to her by Reverend Warren Wilson, she said, 'I do.'

But these are personal delights, pleasures of the flesh and the heart, earthly. The true capacity to love is beyond anything we might receive. I am talking of mystical matters, cosmic importances, spiritual recognitions. Salami might be part of such equations in the holy math of life, but I doubt it.

The world. Probably the first great poem I ever read was during an English exam in the sixth form. It was by Allen Ginsberg, about mooching around a railyard and seeing an ugly yellow flower with a 'soiled dry centre cotton tuft like a used shaving brush that's been lying under the garage for a year'. And then he writes, 'Tough spiky ugly flower, flower nonetheless, with the form of the great yellow rose in your brain! This is the flower of the world.' Yes.

Suffering. Famously, at the end of Graham Greene's novel *Brighton Rock*, a gentle, sneezing priest says, 'You can't conceive, my child, nor can I or anyone, the appalling strangeness of the mercy of God.'

Jesus. Every time there's any kind of theological debate in New Zealand, Presbyterian academics Professor Lloyd Geering and

Professor Jim Veitch are wheeled out to say Jesus taught good things and that, but he was just a man, not the son of God, and he did not rise from the dead, and I wish to hell they'd both piss off.

God. When we die, we are apparently no more than dry sticks in a basket, but you never know.

BIRDS OF A LETTER

PAIGE OF CAMBRIDGE is six years old, and an artist. She has sent me a painting of a thick brown tree like a smoking chimney, and fields, and an orange sun, and a fat, blue, hovering bird, and the title of her work is, 'I Am Very Interested About Birds'. Paige is a deserving winner of our competition to win a free copy of David Attenborough's handsome book *The Life of Birds*.

The rules were simple. In a recent issue, I asked readers to name their favourite bird and explain why. There could be only five winners. We got 187 replies fluttering in from all directions: the rules had touched on something simple and dazzling among these correspondents, who confessed, who declared, who gave memory and yearning the shape of all kinds of birds. They wanted a free book. They broke my heart.

I took the box of envelopes and asked a sensitive colleague to help examine the contents. We were left with an immediate shortlist of 47. From there I went away and perched upon the red velvet couch in my office, where the letters were left to my appalling mercy. The list shrank to 23. And then 17. Then nine. Seven. Six. Five.

The countdown was complete; it had taken two, maybe three hours – there was no way I could take the responsibility at all lightly – in which you could say I became a birdbrain.

What did these appeals say about the hearts and minds of New Zealanders? At least 186 replies were sincere; the admittedly excellent recipe for roast duck, sent in by a rogue from Greymouth, seemed a tad perverse. Many displayed a love for the nearby by voting for the fantail, the kea, the absurd pukeko. Few were exotic, or outrageous: where was the lammergeyer (a bearded vulture found in remote mountain ranges from Spain to China), the dear old archaeopteryx (a transitional fossil between dinosaurs and birds) or the dactlyopterus (a flying fish)?

But there was plenty of imagination. 'The puffin, because they are so crazy looking as if a small child wrote them,' wrote Charles from Mt Maunganui, who enclosed his business card – he has a DipBS in financial planning. Mark from Gisborne sent a remarkable three-page letter about hawks, kingfishers, tui, blue herons, gannets and death, which began, 'When I was a kid I kept a pair of togs under my pillow in case of the Big One.' Interesting. Jocelyn of Christchurch gave geese a stern warning: 'An evolutionary backwater awaits unless they can learn to keep their beaks, with judicious silence, out of bigger birds' business.'

All worthy winners. So, too, was Sarah of Nelson, who voted for galahs. 'Why: Colouring, stupidity.' Black herons got the nod from Patricia of Napier. She envied these fellows. 'When the world gets too much for me,' she wrote, 'I could retreat to the dimness beneath that outstretched parasol of my wings.' Bernadette of Papakura was also moved to poetry with her startling memory of a barn owl. 'I was out walking my dog when a white shape appeared . . . It glided past my face, and away. It was just as though a white cloth was being pulled along a line . . . This was one of the special experiences of my life.'

Peg of Pahiatua quoted author Shonagh Koea when she wondered whether 'the souls of loved cats become fantails'. Mary Anne of Papatoetoe wrote about the cuckoos that were pulverised against the large windows of her house: 'It must have been built in their flightpath. I used to pick them up and massage their necks gently and let them go. I did not have one death.'

We all know nature has no morality. Eric of Taradale cackled about the cockatoo that nearly savaged his brother; Philip, aged five and a half, of Blenheim, drew a peregrin falcon, 'which has killed a pigeon and is eating the pigeon'. More sweetly, four-year-old Jessica of Masterton sent in a priceless photo of herself cuddling a hen, while Jan wrote about her daughter Kirsten dressing a couple of Rhode Island reds up in dolls' clothes and trolleying them through the streets of Newtown.

Brilliant, hilarious, moving, wondrous. I'm sorry the cut came down to only five winners – Lloyd of Dunedin, a bellbird man, who enclosed a newspaper obituary ('Librarian with endearing personality') of his wife Bettina; Paddy of Papakura, whose close encounters with ducks made compelling reading; George of New Plymouth, a fan of blackbirds, who said he would donate the book to the Inglewood Primary School for its refurbished library; Patricia of Sumner, whose wartime memories of Tommy the budgie were tragic in the extreme; and of course Paige, who went straight to the heart of the matter by saying in her covering note, 'I like all the birds in the world.' I like you a lot, Paige.

8 May 1999

ZEKE HERBERT

THEY CALL IT the winterless north, but the skies chundered with rain in Warkworth, and Wellsford, and Whangarei, and Kawakawa, all the way to Kerikeri, that prosperous, deathless town, which the locals, possibly dazed by so much legendary summer, prefer to call Keri. They said, 'Are you from Keri?' And, 'Are you staying in Keri?' No, and definitely no. The main street has computer stores and holiday shoppes, sells antiques and meditation exercises, and an art exhibition promises 'a journey into feminine sculpture'. This is the worst kind of New Zealand, with its filthy lucre, its garishness, its desperate attempt to come across as Queenstown by the sea. It suited the monstrous ego of Zeke Herbert.

His existence has passed happily unnoticed outside of Keri for many years. But the invitation to visit him was too attractive: 'Come for a cup of tea at my humble home and listen for yourself to my album, *A Proper Herbert*, which I'm sure you'll agree is a perfect gift this Christmas. Beautiful music. Sentimental favourites and surprising choices. Personally chosen. Compact disc and tape . . . I am 78 years old and do not have long to live.'

It was no more and no less than a cry for help. As such, on a wet Tuesday afternoon in early December, I knocked on the door of his 'humble home' – a yellow and ochre Spanish-style ranch house decorated, inevitably, with a Sky digital satellite dish – and was met by an old guy wearing a wig. You could tell it was a wig because it jogged on his head as he pumped my hand.

'Pleased to meet you, Chris!' he bellowed.

'The name's Steve,' I corrected.

'Good boy! Enter!'

There were framed photographs of him all along the hallway – it was like seeing his whole life flash before your eyes. Photos of Zeke as a baby, as a sulking schoolboy, as a teenager, on his wedding day (all that remained of his wife was her shoulder), in a tuxedo outside Government House, in a clown suit at Auckland Zoo . . . He grew smaller and balder, the smile wider, the eyes more manic as the photos continued, until all there was left was Zeke in the flesh. Frail, jittery, stooped, wearing a maroon cardigan, check pants and bedroom slippers, he plugged in the electric jug and made good his promise of tea.

'How do you like it, Chris?' he shouted.

'Milk, no sugar.'

'Black it is!'

I sat at the dining room table. He had already set out a tin of shortbread and a sack of sugar. Also, inside a glass, there was a set of false teeth. They grinned wolfishly back at me as Zeke kept up a running monologue from the kitchen: 'Cups. Saucers. That's the ticket. Boil jug. Tea. Something else. Hmmm. Ah! Spoons. That's what we need. Spoons. Where are the spoons? Must have spoons. Now, what's this? Knives. Forks. Pills. No spoons! Honestly, sometimes I don't know whether I'm Arthur . . . or . . . or . . . Arthur.'

Twenty minutes dragged by. Finally, he found a soup ladle, and shovelled three sugars into my tea. 'Now, Chris,' he said. 'Open your notebook. Good boy. Right. I was born in 1922 in Herbertville . . . ' He proceeded to tell me the story of his life. Highlights? Cairo, 1944: 'She handed me something in her closed fist. It was my underwear. Couldn't understand a word she said. Bloody fuzzy-wuzzies.' Wellington, 1967: 'Why she left me, I'll never know. Hurts to this day. Lovely woman. Jill, her name was. Or was it Florence?'

Auckland, 1982: 'Retired. They gave me a gold watch. Lovely. I thought, "I won't know what to do with myself." Still don't.' Kerikeri, 1993: 'Moved up here. Better for my health. Except I have a bad heart, high blood pressure, and the old waterworks aren't too tidy. I also have a sore foot. And my head hurts. I don't hear too well. I'm hungry . . . '

What it amounted to is that Zeke Herbert had worked for State Insurance, rose to senior management, made a pile and retired to Kerikeri, where he was slowly going mad. This was hardly a respectable showbiz bio. I prepared myself for the worst when he decided it was time to play his CD. The opening song was a cover version of the Demis Roussos classic, 'My Friend the Wind'. Stunningly, though, it was a sensitive, faithful interpretation, and Zeke's voice fairly soared out of the speakers, high, wide and handsome.

And then he abruptly turned it off. 'Oh dear,' he said. 'Sorry about that! I'm playing you the original version.'

While he fumbled around looking for his own CD, I asked him – and it was tiring to have to shout at such a throat-shredding volume – whether he had any background in entertainment whatsoever.

'My word, yes,' he said. 'I've been quite the star in my time. Ham radio for 14 years. Once recognised myself in a street scene on the six o'clock TV news. As for my live work, I used to play the spoons at an old folks' home. I was a hit with the old dears, let me tell you! But . . . ' He sat down and began to weep. I gave his shoulder a comforting squeeze. 'Oh, Chris,' he sniffled. 'Wherever did I put the spoons?' And then he began to howl.

The poor wretch needed to be alone with his grief, so I tiptoed out of the room and onto the front porch. A breeze flapped at his longjohns on the clothesline. The rain fell softly now, and the sky had a pale, unwell colour. I thought about how every New Zealand summer has days like this, sometimes on Christmas Day itself – rain, and a light wind, and moping clouds, a sense of disappointment in the close, sticky air, even a resentment about living in this dump in the South Pacific. In desperation, some of us watch TV, and there's never anything on. Others stray outside, dragging their heels, squinting at the white sky, irritated by sandflies, barking dogs, the dull porridge of sand. The occasion has fallen flat. Life is put on hold. There is a tyre in the creek, a broken kite stuffed in a litter bin, a rat up a drainpipe . . .

'Chris!' bellowed the old fool, his voice cheerful once more. 'Chris! Yoo-hoo!'

He had found his CD. It was time to face the music. *A Proper Herbert* featured 12 tracks, opening with 'My Friend the Wind' and closing with 'Candle in the Wind'. It was excruciating, idiotic, a massacre. Its only possible virtue was if Herbert had intended the whole thing as a comedy album – track five was a version of David Bowie's 'Laughing Gnome'. But when it finished, he said, 'I chose that for the melody.'

His voice was reedy, cracked, yowling. He forgot the words to some of the songs – 'Lady in Red' changed in mid-chorus to 'Lady in Blue'. Instead of singing, he spoke the lyrics to 'The Wind Beneath my Wings'. He made a complete hash of 'Poi E'.

On and on it went, but the musical backing was at least competent, even professional. In between 'Rock me Amadeus' and 'Every Rose Has Its Thorn', I commented on this, and he said, 'Got some wallah in. Paid him. Did a good job, I suppose. His name? Oh, for the life me, I can't remember . . . Maurice, or something . . . '

The experience of meeting him and listening to his abominable record was, in fact, touching. He definitely needed help. I gave him what I could, something that he also craved: company, attention, publicity. The faded portraits in his hallway, that screeching voice on CD, the fact he had sewn his initials onto his clothes . . . He was his own spinning world, but he could be capable of small acts of kindness – the biscuits, the sweet tea. Watching him nod off in the middle of his version of 'Mull of Kintyre' filled me with compassion for this strange creature of Keri.

He woke suddenly, and shouted, 'Well, young fellow, what do you think, eh? Speak up!'

I hummed and hahed for a while, and he boomed, 'I know your game! You're a bloody critic! Oh, don't you think I don't know what people like you think! I'm expecting some bad reviews from you lot! Critics – pah! Envious, bitter little people! Lower than apes! Ectoplasms! Bashi-bazouks! Sea gherkins! Pirates! Heretics! Vegetarians!'

The madman continued to rave while I stood up, thanked him for his time and said goodbye. It was dark outside. As I walked to the gate, I noticed something shining in his letterbox. I stopped to see what had caught the moonlight.

I had found Zeke Herbert's spoons.

8 January 2001

THE TRUTH ABOUT ZEKE HERBERT

THE TRUTH about Zeke Herbert is really fairly obvious. A number of *Listener* readers wrote in saying they were quick to cotton on to the fact that Zeke was a thinly concealed portrait of some bloke on TV who had just released an appalling album of 'sentimental favourites'. Only a few people were caught out, like Judy of Hamilton, who emailed to say how 'offended' she was by the 'rude and bullying' way I treated poor, mad Zeke, while someone from the Kerikeri newspaper *Chronicle* interviewed me over the phone to ask for Zeke's number, and to wonder why I hated that lousy town so much.

The subsequent story, 'Listener Critic Gives Kerikeri Big Thumbs Down', asked the burning question: 'Who is Steve Braunias that he should have such a jaundiced view of Kerikeri?' The vague answer: 'Steve was totally unaware of the *North & South* top town award won by Kerikeri when contacted at the *Listener* offices. He was not at all disturbed to find his view so diametrically opposed. He said disdainfully that he probably wouldn't agree with *North & South* about many things. So what specifically didn't he like about Kerikeri? "It's the worst town. It's the vibe – plastic, sort of too Christian," he said, vaguely.'

I hate coming across as dim, sour and charmless, which is why I rarely consent to give interviews. I promised, vaguely, that I would call Zeke and ask him to contact the newspaper. The story ended: 'And who is Zeke Herbert? Don't know at this stage. We'll let you know when we track him down.'

But my Zeke article was much less a hoax than a simple parody of a TV star with a stink voice. There were all sorts of clues. His willingness to bang on about his ill health. The reference to 'ham radio'. A particularly famous quote – really, there is a case to be made that he came up with the Great New Zealand Punchline: 'She handed me something in her closed fist. It was underwear.' Another quote ('I chose that for the melody') was a straight lift from an interview he gave to the *Woman's Weekly*. His hatred of critics, his clown suit. The whole entire folly of lending his 'reedy, cracked, yowling howl' to an album of innocent songs.

How transparent. It was the same as when I wrote a simple parody of the same TV star who had just published a stink autobiography. This time around, he is disguised as Hulmes, a bankteller with a 'monstrous sense of self-regard' who distinguishes himself as a 'fantasist and a fabulist of rare distinction'. There is that priceless literary classic again: 'She handed me something in her closed fist. It was her underwear.' His quote about Bobo Rulston ('I freely acknowledge his huge abilities. Bobo often risks it all . . . Customers love the sense of danger') is a direct lift from Bill Ralston's *Metro* cover story on the guy. And there are the references to Liz Gunn, Mike Hosking, Beaver, Muffy, Pussy, Foo-Foo, and 'the marriage to his beloved Bugsy'.

Similarly, there was at least an attempt at betraying my real feelings for him (Zeke Herbert is 'kind', and meeting him is 'touching'; Hulmes is 'at heart . . . likeable and harmless'), because the TV star in question is actually a good man with a big heart. The first time I met him, we crowded into a taxivan with a pack of drunken idiots, and he insisted on getting out to help a disabled woman into the passenger seat. Later, he came to my birthday party, and we hooked up at a waterfront bar on his birthday. I always found him to be bright, generous and charming, qualities that I possess in my dreams. He knew the cut of my cloth, he knew what

I was capable of. 'There is absolutely no way in the world I'd ever let you interview me!' he merrily hooted over a drink on a couple of occasions, and I merrily hooted, too. We were a pair of merry hooters back then.

You will not be astonished to learn that we have never spoken since I wrote the 'Hulmes' parody. Such are the casual betrayals of a columnist who cannot resist selling 850 words of flesh.

Still, the guy did write a lousy book and record a lousy album. And apart from regret that our friendship was nipped in the bud, I have to admit that my main concern was that he would reach for his lawyer. Satire is no defence. Which is why I fired through the 'Hulmes' parody to the *Listener* lawyers before the column went to press. They faxed back a reply along the lines that it was perfectly fine, no worries, proceed with a light heart.

I followed up with a phone call.

'Are you sure?' I asked.

'Oh, yes,' said the lawyer. 'You've expressed a fair opinion.'

'That's good, then,' I said.

'Yes,' she said. 'By the way, which bank does this guy Hulmes work in?'

Long pause.

'You do realise', I said, 'the column is actually about Paul Holmes?'

Really long pause.

I never did get around to faxing her to check the Zeke Herbert interview.

HERE ARE some facts about Barry Moore: he is 24, lives in Hamilton East, has a snake-hipped frame, and is a total legend, famous for 15 minutes every quarter of an hour in his chosen field. A god, almost, a champion, officially. This month, he heads for Detroit, to represent New Zealand – Moore won the national title for the third year running on a turbulent Petone night just before Christmas – in the 2000 Air Guitar World Cup. 'I'm gonna rock for New Zealand!' he hollers.

Air guitar – you won't find it in any dictionary of musical terms, but it's an art, possibly, and it's widely practised, definitely. An air guitarist is that guy you see at parties. He's on the dance floor, and there's some hard rock playing on the stereo, and he's pretending to fire off all those hot riffs and blistering solos. He's out of it. Also, he's into it: 'No one can stop me,' says Moore, 'when I'm in the mood.'

Fair warning. But how the hell did this ever become an internationally recognised event? Mime is bad enough, but air guitaring? Absurd, preposterous – well, until Moore digs out his invitation to Detroit. The trip is all expenses paid: the travel, the accommodation (Holiday Inn), the meals. There are 40 finalists, from Germany, Egypt, Australia, even Burkina Faso. ('Never underestimate the Africans,' Moore advises.) First prize, US$35,000.

In that case, pray continue. 'I first got into air guitar properly at the Gunners gig in '91,' he begins. Moore means the Guns N' Roses concert in Auckland. He only had eyes for lead guitarist Slash. 'His moves – awesome, man. Legs apart. The windmill arm action. The positioning of his axe.' Moore played along to Slash for the entire show. 'I was always a few seconds behind him, obviously, but all my mates who were there with me were just blown away at my performance.'

He also attracted the attention of a visitor from the Hawke's Bay. 'This guy from Napier comes up to me, and says, "You've got what it takes." And then he told me about the wonderful world,' Moore smiles, ducking his head a little, 'of competitive air guitar.'

And soon he was on the road in his Triumph, attending air guitar battles in Napier, Tauranga, Wellington, Whangarei, Blenheim, Christchurch and, once, in Invercargill: 'Once was enough! They're all into air speed metal down there. No finesse.'

Moore's own repertoire grew as he improved. He mastered Slash, then Dinosaur Jnr, Nirvana, Smashing Pumpkins, Straitjacket Fits. 'And then I discovered old school.' He means the 1970s, the high tide of rock guitar, when behemoths such as Peter Frampton and Eddie Van Halen strode the earth. In 1997, in Upper Hutt, he won his first national title with his airing of Van Halen's 'You Really Got Me'. His two victory performances since then were 'Voodoo Chile' by Jimi Hendrix and 'Dazed and Confused' by Led Zeppelin, in which Moore faithfully sawed his air guitar with a violin bow, and even played notes backwards.

Remarkable. He is the subject of intense adoration in fanzines and on Internet sites: his audience in Petone last month were so uplifted they wrecked the stage: copies of his exhibition video *NZ On Air* are studied in the US, and he is 'big in Japan'. Still, it's unlikely that the guy will ever make an air record, and real musicians sneer at him.

'A good air guitarist is better than a bad real guitarist,' he claims. 'In Rotorua a few months ago, I played at a private party, right, and everyone was pretty loose, so I thought I'd try out something I'd been working on at home – I put on the Eagles' "Hotel California", but when it got to the solo, I turned the stereo off and kept playing. Right? No music, just me on air. No one knew what to think for a few seconds, but then someone says, "I can hear him playing!" And then everyone got into it. They could see by looking at the expressions on my face, and the way my hands moved, that I was doing a note-perfect solo. One guy even yelled out, "Turn it down!" That was a fantastic night, man.'

He's planning to pull the same stunt in Detroit. There are four heats before judges decide on quarter-final places; Moore's other pieces are likely to include the full 13-minute version of 'Do You Feel Like We Do' by Peter Frampton, Ted Nugent's 'Wang Dang Sweet Poontang' and, as a patriotic gesture, the *Country Calendar* theme tune. 'I'm worried about what cowboy hat to wear,' he frets.

The interview took place in his bedroom, Moore's HQ during all the years he has perfected his curious ability. 'People might think, "He should get out of the house more!" It's hard to gain respect sometimes for what I do.' But he works as a data processor, lives with his girlfriend Maxine, and voted Labour in the election. 'Boring, really. But I'm happy.'

But then this pleasant, ordinary New Zealander accepts a request to play some air guitar, and he turns on an old favourite, 'November Rain' by Guns N' Roses, and suddenly Barry Moore is Slash, his legs open, eyes closed, mouth twisted into painful, ecstatic grimaces, as he smashes out huge power chords that ring like really loud bells and chases the screeching guitar solo to the ends of the earth. And you watch, astonished, and notice that he has such beautiful hands.

8 January 2000

THE TRUTH ABOUT BARRY MOORE

OUR 8 JANUARY issue this year included a story I wrote about three-time New Zealand air guitar champion Barry Moore. An air guitarist, the story helpfully explained, 'is that guy you see at parties. He's on the dance floor, and there's some hard rock playing on the stereo, and he's pretending to fire off all these hot riffs and blistering solos'. Moore was 'big in Japan'; he air guitared to songs by Led Zeppelin and Straitjacket Fits; he had released an exhibition video called *NZ On Air*. 'No one can stop me when I'm in the mood,' said Moore, a 24-year-old data processor who lived with his girlfriend Maxine in Hamilton East. He was about to fly to Detroit to represent New Zealand in the 2000 Air Guitar World Cup, up against 40 finalists 'from Germany, Egypt, Australia, even Burkina Faso' for the first prize of $35,000. He had 'such beautiful hands'.

I made it all up. Superbly, though, it conned some of the biggest names in New Zealand show business, and you bet I gleefully reported each and every invitation for Barry to perform to our designer Derek Ward – he had posed for the photographs. But like all hoaxes, it eventually went too far . . .

Things started innocently enough, when Bruce from the *Waikato Times* called to ask for Barry's number – he was astonished the *Listener* had scooped the story from his own back yard. I told Bruce I'd pass on his request to Barry, and left it at that. In the meantime, I received a long, rambling letter from Michael of Radio One in Dunedin. 'Moore was right when he pointed out that a good air guitarist is better than bad real guitarist . . . It's the pose, the strut, the pelvic grind that counts . . . I have to concede there's a degree of skill in air guitaring without a prop such as a tennis racquet. The minimum I ever managed with was a breadboard.' Yes.

A few weeks later, this email came from a TV director called Bill: 'Re the wonderful story you wrote about the air guitar chap. I'm lucky enough to be accompanying Mikey Havoc and Jeremy Wells on a jaunt around and about New Zealand, and we thought we could go and see him. Do you have his address? Yours sincerely . . . ' I wrote a reply saying that Barry would agree to be filmed only if he could have Havoc's red jersey. I have no idea whether Havoc even has a red jersey, but it sounded like something Barry would want. I deleted the message, though, and sincerely admitted it was all complete bullshit. Bill wrote back, 'You definitely had us all going with that story. We all feel slightly shorter and less clever today.'

Well, where *Havoc* goes, *Ice TV* always follows. 'What an interesting subject!' emailed Heidi from production, inviting Barry to perform. In reply, I rather brutally told her he had died in a road accident – he had smashed his Triumph while driving to perform in an air guitar event in Mosgiel.

In March, Glenys emailed to invite Barry to perform at a work function in Hamilton East. Deciding that he was still alive, I asked whether Barry might get paid. I aimed high: $25. No problem, she said; he could also help himself to free drinks and barbecued food. 'The thing is,' she added, 'we are having the social club function tonight. I have been trying for a couple of weeks to track him down through local radio stations, but although they were really interested that such a person existed, they hadn't heard of him.' Regretfully, I had to tell her it was too short notice for the maestro to perform, but he appreciated the offer of a hot sausage.

Next up was an email from a TV director called Sean. 'We're in pre-production for a new TV show featuring the magnificent Gary McCormick. The show is called *McCormick Rips*, and involves Gary

117

performing live around the country with special guests from the area. To this end, we would like Barry Moore to be one of our guests in Cambridge.' Such a shame, I told Sean, but Barry was attending a funeral – his own? – in Mosgiel that day. It strikes me now that Barry might well have saved *McCormick Rips* from being canned after two shows.

And then it turned nasty. Barry was asked to play at Sound 2000, a musical equipment expo held at Auckland's Aotea Centre. The expo's PR, Angela, offered $50, but during two emails expressed sarcastic doubt that Barry existed. This was no way to treat a legend. 'Barry and I find your tone offensive and insulting,' I replied. 'I don't know what your fucking problem is . . . The invitation is rejected.' She phoned up in a hell of a temper, and we swore at each other, and then her boss called and profusely apologised, and said he'd given Angela a bollocking for her behaviour . . .

Sorry, Angela. You were the smartest of the lot. It's obviously time to call a halt to the hoax; too bad, though, that I never got around to applying to New Zealand On Air to fund a TV documentary about Barry. The chances are high that they would have paid.

8 July 2000

MYRNA & COSTA

JOURNALISM IS the first refuge of scoundrels: everyone knows the profession is venal, uncouth, morally corrupt: too right I like it. It pays you all right. You get to travel. Chance and bad judging mean you can win the occasional award. You learn a great deal about a great many subjects, even though you usually forget everything a week or two after each story is published; interviews are a strange, low art, and you can sometimes come up with a nice sentence. And because the trade is a public service, there is opportunity to do a power of good for others.

But very often readers of this column will write to me and heartily recommend I take the first train out of journalism. They have my interests at heart. They want me to better myself. They want me to write fiction. They assume I will write fiction, they predict I will write fiction, they demand I write fiction. I take their point. What I do for a living is a humble little craft of passing interest; fiction swoops, leaps, lasts, reaches the places journalism can never find. And every time I am told this is where I really ought to go, I think, *Why should I want to do that?*

It's much harder work. The pages are entirely at your disposal and absolutely insatiable. You have to feed them characters, plots, dialogue, themes, action, thought, and everything else lying around on the shelves of the foul rag-and-bone shop of your heart and soul. I know about these things. The fact is I have written quite a lot of fiction, all of it published, all of it ridiculous.

In 1999, the *Dominion* exposed my use of a fictonal line-up of reviewers during my time as the editor of *Capital Times* in

Wellington. What the story didn't mention is that I also invented two short story writers: Costa Levin (note the lame pun) and his niece Myrna Levin. Both wrote serialised fiction for the newspaper: Costa was later published in the *Sunday Star-Times*; the prolific Myrna in *RTR Countdown, More, Metro* and the *Listener*. Neither as far as I am aware has ever been referenced in any guide to New Zealand literature.

A shame. They had their moments. Their existence at *Capital Times* came from my great desire for fiction to reflect current events, current places, current weather; famously, Dickens and Chekhov wrote in this manner, commissioned by newspapers to write daily instalments which would play off whatever was happening in London or St Petersburg. The Levins were not fit to fill the inkpots of Dickens or Chekhov, but their stories at least had the vigour to travel all over the shop in Wellington. The hero of Costa's six-week series 'Blue Tuesday' zipped from the shooting range in Breaker Bay to the tunnels on Mt Kaukau, the rubbish tip at Happy Valley to enjoying 'an hour's nap in the queue at the Willis Street post office'.

Myrna wrote a lot about sex, and so her stories featured a lot of sex in Wellington. The heroine of her four-week series 'Blues for Billy Red' begins with her picking up a foreign bloke at Clare's Nightclub (my idea of a current event: they dance to New Order and Prince) and taking him home to her apartment in Oriental Parade. They later have sex on top of Mt Victoria, in the stands at the Basin Reserve, at Glover Park in Vivien Street and the beach at Makara, and then she kills him in her bathtub and puts the body in a wheelbarrow and waits until night to trundle him to the wharf where she tips him out by the Cook Strait ferry terminal. I think I may have mentioned my fiction is ridiculous.

The central conceit of publishing my own fiction reached its properly absurd conclusion: in my final issue as editor, I put Myrna on the cover – it was good of my friend Caroline Pilbrow to agree to pose as the author – and featured an 800-word interview with her. Q: Why are your stories so concerned with death, deceit and melodrama? A: 'Because I'm a deeply sensitive woman with a lurid imagination, and a shallow understanding of life. How about that?'

Myrna's reappearance in *Metro* saw her doing for Auckland what she had done for Wellington. Her six-month serial 'Mr Collins' really got around, and 'reported' on the city from all sorts of places – her hero was buttfucked in Devonport, Point Chevalier, Papakura, Glen Innes, Helensville and the entrance to Kaipara Harbour at South Head peninsula. Poor devil. Outside of inflicting these outrages on Collins, I did try to give a sense of Auckland life. Mostly by buying things. The theme, if anyone asked, was Auckland's culture of consumption. Collins buys a 3-D clock of the Last Supper for $39.95 at the China Emporium on Dominion Road, forks out $29.95 at Bizarre Beats on Karangahape Road for an imported CD of *Sweet Apology of Death* by Morgue, and spends a further $5 at the Waterfront Beach Camp Store in Muriwai for a stainless-steel Tramontina fish-gutting knife, which he uses to kill and then eat gannets on Motutara Island.

How bad was it? Keri Hulme wrote to the magazine and gave of her opinion: 'Dear Myrna. I am not at all sure you're a woman (I suspect you may be a committee), but I have no doubts about the quality of your writing. It's crud.'

Yes. You can blame Bill Ralston. When he was appointed editor of *Metro*, Bill took me to lunch at Kwan's Thai restaurant (you should go there at once), and chatted me up to join the magazine as a staff writer. This was confusing, because I had just received a similar offer from the *Listener*. What to do? Bill's pitch, though, was irresistible. He wanted me to write serial fiction which would reflect

121

current events, current places, current weather . . .

I joined the *Listener* two years later. Myrna made what will probably be her last comeback when I gave her my column in the 7 August 1999 issue. It was a story about a travelling salesman who is stopped by a woman waving frantically by the roadside near Te Kuiti. She tells him her husband has died. They drive to the house. She weeps, and pours out two glasses of whiskey. And then another two, and another two, and they dance to 'My Funny Valentine', and they kiss, but then she pushes him away and asks him to help her dress the body.

Two responses. A woman called Lindsay called the *Listener*'s arts editor Margo White to say she was a film-maker, was interested in co-writing a project with Myrna, and did Margo know her contact details? Another reader ripped the story out of the magazine, and mailed it to me with a comment in blue felt-tip angrily scrawled all over the page. It read, 'What an awfully stupid lot of writing this is! Awfully bad.' A line at the end of the story advised readers that I was on leave. My correspondent had added, and too right I totally agree with the sentiment, 'Great pity! Bring back Steve Braunias.'

DINNER PARTY

IT WAS AN honour to be invited to the Vernon home for dinner. There was his immense wealth, and her fame: they knew the right politicians, and the left media: when they walked together into a room, there was always a man who squared his shoulders and a woman who began whispering to her friend. Their generosity could save your life – hospitals, shelters, medical research. They had excellent taste – their children, their cars, their artwork. Deborah Vernon had just bought a Bill Hammond painting. She didn't like it very much, but was convinced about its importance by Robert Green, the young curator at the gallery who had talked her out of buying a Shane Cotton, which she really didn't like in the slightest but thought *might* be important.

'Come over next Friday,' she said. 'We're having a few people around. Just a small meal. Would you?'

Robert showed up at the house at eight. Although the dark sky began to spit, he was so nervous he parked outside their gate on the street. The house was really a mansion, part Spanish and part Tudor, hidden behind trees and set back towards the sea. There were a couple of small sheds on the front property, and a rabbit hutch. There was a tall railing around the entire section.

The maximum security put Robert in a state of maximum insecurity. He had a new haircut at Servilles, especially for the occasion, but he was alarmed by the pinch that a clothes peg had put in the shoulder of his nice white shirt from Workshop, and he was sure that his Ego aftershave smelled like vinegar. His heeled Italian shoes only made him feel short.

'Come on in, little fellow!' boomed Leslie Vernon, who opened the door wearing a peasant shirt which had cost him $950. 'Ah, here's Deborah.'

'Oh, how good you could make it, Richard,' she said. 'May I take your jacket?'

'No, please,' said Robert. 'I mean, no, thanks.'

He was taken through to the other guests. There was an ex-All Black, a TV newsreader, four lawyers, three MPs, two convicts, a woman from a women's magazine, and a man who owned a chain of menswear. 'I'm sure you've heard of everyone,' said Leslie.

Be cool, thought Robert. He shook hands with the newsreader, and asked wittily, 'What do you do?' The newsreader said, 'What don't I?' and walked away. He stood beside the women's magazine woman and one of the lawyers. After a few minutes, the woman turned and looked at him, and brushed his shoulder. 'Dandruff,' she said. 'Or was that salt to go with your vinegar?'

Morosely, he stationed himself at the hors d'oeuvres table. There were 12 dozen fresh oysters, four crayfish and 18 whitebait fritters. 'Sea food and eat it,' said the ex-All Black. Robert waited too long to laugh, and was alone again.

He found the Hammond painting, and stood admiring it for eight minutes, hoping someone would be drawn to him. Leslie Vernon finally approached. 'What do you think?' he asked.

'Well – '

'Do you think it needs a frame?'

Robert said no, it didn't. Righto, said his host, and told him to sit down at the dinner table.

They ate avocados, sole meunière, Chateaubriand, and chilled fresh strawberries with rich cream and a spoonful of kirsch. There were also chicken pieces coated in egg and breadcrumbs and fried slowly in a quantity of butter and herbs. 'Delicious,' said Robert, and that was the only thing he said during dinner. He blushed so much that he began to sweat. He sat a little too far away from the table, but was too afraid to move his chair closer. The voices of the guests babbled over the plates and in his ears.

Immediately after the small meal, he thanked Leslie and Deborah Vernon for a nice evening. As they showed him the door, he heard the women's magazine woman saying, 'I call her the Foghorn of Canton!'

It was now raining very hard; there was a heavy storm, with thunder, and lightning, and the wind shook the trees by their throats. Robert was soaking wet within two minutes. He had a pounding headache. He looked behind him at the house, where every window seemed lit behind the curtains. What a humiliating dinner party that was! The guests hated him: the Vernons obviously regretted inviting him: he was out of his league, struck dumb, badly dressed, a bore, an idiot, a nobody, unworldly, short.

He stumbled against the rabbit hutch, tried to cower from the rain in a doorway of a shed. The storm exhausted him. He walked into the railing and held onto its cold, wet bars like some dramatic figure in a bad film. There were shrubs everywhere. He turned around to the back of the house and looked out to the black water smashing against the cliff.

Fully three-quarters of an hour after he had left the house, soaked and ravaged, Robert knocked on the front door. Nobody heard him. He banged against it with both fists. Leslie Vernon opened the door and looked at him with his mouth open. Behind him, Robert could see the women's magazine woman naked, holding a leash around the ex-All Black's neck.

'Excuse me,' said Robert, 'but I couldn't find the gate.'

4 November 2000

POLITICAL DIARY

LAST SUNDAY, the morning after election night, I fossicked through my tin trunk of personal documents – love letters, birthday cards, school reports, unpaid bills dating back to 1981 – to find pages of a diary which recorded Labour's win in 1984. I wanted to know what it felt like back then. At the time, I was working at Victoria University's religious studies department, in a villa shared with philosophy department staff, where I researched a history of various orphanages and old folks' homes run by the Presbyterian church.

17 JULY

At midday there were four academics standing in my office listening in silence to the radio news about our 'currency crisis'. It was raining outside and the sky was black, and I said, 'Dark days, eh,' and a philosophy lecturer said, 'It's like the war's been announced.' As the news trailed off so did the academics and I switched stations.

It's been all political high drama ever since the snap election announced on 14 June, and the election night itself on Saturday night. I cast my vote for the first time, at the Municipal Electricity Department in Webb Street. I went for Labour and Prohibition. Afterwards I walked over to my drug dealer's house and gave him $30. The drug dealer and his brother said they voted Labour, too. I live in a Labour district and part of a completely Labour city as it turned out.

I enjoyed the campaign. All the philosophers and religious studiers talked about it. My favourite TV shows were rescheduled because of nightly party political broadcasts by Muldoon, Lange

126

and Jones. Lange kept saying, 'Let's look at the facts', and 'When we open the books', and 'We've had enough!'

Coming back from lunch at the Hob coffee lounge the day before the election, I saw four cars driving down Kelburn Parade festooned with New Zealand Party streamers and someone squawking out something about Bob Jones on a megaphone. A house on the Terrace with placards for NZ First candidate John Feast was paintbombed that afternoon. A shame. At 5am one day last week I got up and drew Feast's nose into the shape of a dripping tap.

Later on election day, I mooched along the wharves and looked at ashtrays made of crabshells in the Nautical Museum. Back home I lit a coal fire and watched a film on TV that night. Little messages raced across the screen giving the latest election results. Labour was winning most.

Gary rang to invite me to his place, so I walked over in the rain. I stopped in at a bottle store on Marjoribanks Street for some Waikato XXX and heard on the radio that Labour had become the new government. The next day it rained heavily. I bought a paper and the front-page headline said, IT'S LANGE.

And so now here at work on a Tuesday afternoon, a 'currency crisis', and a philosopher said, 'They should have hung that bastard Muldoon years ago.'

18 JULY

Didn't get much sleep last night because at midnight the neighbours started playing Siouxsie and the Banshees records. I hate Siouxsie and the Banshees records. Finally at 2am I went out to the garden and slung mud at their windows and screamed at them to shut the fuck up.

Lange made a major political decision this morning on Sharon Crosbie's radio programme. I rounded up everyone from philosophy and religious studies, and the campus driver. Lange firstly called

Muldoon a liar and a cheat, and then said the dollar would have a 20 percent devaluation. Naturally, I have no idea what that last part means.

There was immediate discussion afterwards, and morning tea. Professor Lloyd Geering ate more than his share of gingernuts. He always does. I don't like him. George Hughes, ex-chair of philosophy, ran his finger over the empty plate for crumbs. My boss, Reverend Jim Veitch, wore a tweed sportsjacket and scoffed a strawberry yoghurt. I interrupted him to make a financial statement myself: I touched him up for $10 till payday. Went to the Mandarin coffee lounge for lunch and wolfed down a steak.

Back at work, talk was continuing about the devaluation. A religious studier has lost shares because of it. He was in a black mood. I asked Jim if it was really that bad, and he said it was, but that it would all blow over next week. Then we discussed the Book of Revelations. Jim explained that it wasn't, as I thought, a prophetic vision of Armageddon, but a prose-poem of then-contemporary events. I told him about my Siouxsie and the Banshees incident.

19 JULY

The only big political news today is Muldoon's future as leader of National. His caucus met this afternoon to make an announcement this afternoon – it interrupted Philip Liner's *Music for Pleasure* programme. Caucus said Muldoon could stay till the end of the year.

I went through the minutes' book of the Kandhar Home for the Aged. The matron wrote in 16 October 1965, 'Mr Olsen managed to get away from us again. He had climbed out of his window early one morning and was found on Opaki Rd with all his clothes done up in a swag. All he could tell me was that he couldn't find any trace of any pigs.'

11 December 1999

SPRING

ONE OF THE last times I saw my mother was on an afternoon at her home in Mt Maunganui, when she was reading the *Bay of Plenty Times* death notices. Someone she once knew, an old bloke, had got his name published. I said, 'Does it say how he kicked the bucket?' We were drinking from a pot of tea in the sitting room. Mum was in her favourite chair and I sat on the couch, feet up on the electric heater; through the glass sliding doors, you could see the front lawn, flower beds, and for excitement an occasional kid riding a bicycle along dusty Ranch Road. Usually around that time of afternoon you could hear a goods train as it roared past the yellow lupin bushes beside the track which ran behind town. She said, 'It just says, "He died in his sleep at milking time."'

Another notice more soberly gave the time at something like 4am. Death before dawn – a New Zealand way to go, taken out in the dark, the herd meanwhile down in the milking shed, steam rising off their backs, electric light, motors, corrugated iron, the amazing sight of so much milk, white and thick, being sucked through the hoses to the tank. It should smell to low hell of shit and lagoons of piddle, but actually the stink is refreshing, and there is also the sweet, raw tang of milk as drops from the hose spot the concrete.

First things first, though, because the day begins back in bed, where sleep clings like a huge beard to your shocked face as you rise and make your way to the kitchen to put on the kettle and warm your hands on whatever heat remains from last night's stove fire. It's only early spring, but still bloody cold in the mornings, and rain falls from the darkness.

Raincoat, a thick pair of pants, gumboots. The panting dog on the back of your farm bike, you drive to the paddock and urge the herd into action, torchlight blazing holes in the black hills. There's always the same few cows who know the score and wait to set off down the race. Close the gate. For a moment, turn off the torch. Look behind you, and you can't see a thing – the darkness of New Zealand countryside before dawn is the blackest thing you might ever experience. But you can hear the shambling, clicking hooves, and maybe the stream.

Most of the herd should have calved by now. They are up to their ears in milk. The motor is turning over back at the shed, and it's nice to have something playing on the radio; cows hardly deserve to suffer Paul Holmes or Sean Plunket more than anyone else, but Concert FM is perfect until the birds clear their throats.

Any funny business from a kicking, ill-tempered cow and there is soft twine to tie up a back leg. You have to watch for bloat, and mastitis, and infections, and any humping may mean a sudden outbreak of lesbian fever but is more likely a sign of heat and for you to make a note of the eartag and ask the vet to get their arm stuck right in.

Otherwise – gently place the chain over your client's back, get the cups on, click the suction clamp and you're in business. The milk must go through; the world of good, decent citizens who like their coffee white depends on it. Wait till the last drop. Show some mercy and common sense, for heaven's sake, and click the clamp off before you remove the cups. Open the gate – but first, slip off the chain and bar it against the next client or she will barrel on past, right in front of your astonished snoot, and bad language has no place on a farm.

Afterwards, with the cows led to a new pasture, you must

observe cleanliness and rip the shit and piss off the concrete with a high-pressure hose. Good work. It's now past dawn, and you have seen the black sky smudge to grey, the world become visible, the dripping trees, the cat with its tongue out, and taken a look in the milk tank.

Old hands at this game will almost certainly shake their heads and tut at all kinds of mistakes and foolishness in my report of an experience I have enjoyed only once – on my father-in-law's farm in Uruti, in Taranaki. Apologies, but there you have it. I felt baffled, wary of a kick in the chops, alive. I thought of the old bloke who died at milking time, and of my mum, and standing on a church stage at her funeral and saying how she helped out on her dad's farm as a girl in Morrinsville – that morning in Uruti was so vivid, and important, and I kept thinking, *I must remember everything.*

18 September 1999

EVERYONE KNOWS that the best stories in the newspapers are buried in a column usually headlined 'News in brief'. It's here that we find such staggering and random reports that a swarm of bees has stung a flock of geese to death in Germany, that two burglars who appeared before a Zambian magistrate were wearing his shirts, and that a Russian killed his mother and ate her liver after frying it on the stove. Mostly to read up on ancient football reports, I occasionally buy old copies of the *London Daily Mirror*, which used to bind a week's worth of newspapers together and were shipped out to New Zealand; they are a treasure trove of the vivid, trivial, snatched report. 15 July 1954: a briefcase lost in Bolton and sold as lost property had two sandwiches in it. 7 May 1972: four armed men wearing Arsenal shirts robbed a post office of 18,000 pounds on their way to the FA Cup final at Wembley.

And this just in, from Nelson – the opening sentence of a five-paragraph story told in 22 beautifully chosen words, with its Jack-and-Jill monosyllables and its one crucial comma: 'He wanted to lie naked in the sun and drink wine, but ended up surrounded by armed police who shot his dog.'

Bloody hell. At one level, the interesting thing about that sentence is the beauty of its language – in an attempt to influence the future of newspaper reporting, I handed out photocopies to liven up a typically boring lecture I recently gave at a class of journalism students. Cheers to the reporter who crafted that small, shimmering miracle: the dynamic narrative (a nice lie-down shattered by a gunshot) and deep sense of mystery (who called the cops? what dog?) has the brainwave of great art. It may even be the Great New Zealand Sentence.

The rest of the story explained itself in the boring language of journalism – it was based on a case in the District Court. The incident seemed sad, unpleasant, dismal. A 35-year-old man, described as 'harmless' and 'of no fixed abode', stopped by a house which he thought was abandoned, took off his clothes in the yard and got stuck into some wine. 'But the house was not derelict and the occupants called the police . . . The prosecutor said the man's dog was shot because it was savage and had previously injured someone.' The guy was convicted and sentenced to nine months' 'supervision'.

A sorry state of affairs. Quite obviously, the full picture is missing – what was the man's side of the story, what was the dog's side of the story, what it may or may not say about life in Nelson – but the fact of the matter is that I'll remember this story long after the front-page lead with its heavy-inked headline has wandered across my mind and disappeared. Some new crisis in the Clark regime, a dark warning about drug abuse, claims that business confidence is low . . . on 'Morning Report' and the evening news on TV, these solemn and important events go in one ear and out the other.

Always more astonishing is the ordinary chaos of the world. A few winters ago, friends invited me for the weekend at a holiday home in Leigh: someone cooked a big meal, there was an incident on a gentle hill involving vertigo, we had wood-fired baths in the pitch darkness: it was all very pleasant. But what I remember most is reading a small report in the local paper about some poor wretch who was caught masturbating in long grass outside a women's public toilet. He told the judge: 'I think I might have a problem.'

You can almost hear his pitiful, accurate bleat. And while it's true that I don't recall the judgment of the court – although you would have to think the guy was at least given 'supervision' – the poignancy of the event was as memorable as its sordid nature. Again, what it says about life in New Zealand is left to the imagination.

My own favourite as a working journalist involved a charge of assault in the District Court at Greymouth. It came just after a case where two blokes were had up for shaving a forestry worker's eyebrows while he was asleep – 'It's just about a West Coast tradition,' reckoned one of the guilty men. 'He who falls asleep loses an eyebrow.' This kept me wide awake at all times. Anyway, it was then the turn of a guy to plead guilty to hitting a woman at a party. The night after he had helped to sandbag Greymouth wharf during a flood, he got boozed at a party, belted a woman, and her boyfriend stepped in and kicked him in the head and threw him against a potbelly stove; he suffered second-degree burns. Not good. But why did he hit the woman in the first place? Because she treated his dog 'in a bizarre and unacceptable fashion'. She had masturbated it. What this says about a dog's life in New Zealand is unclear, but the woman had clearly gone too far, and the guilty man's lawyer told the judge – this is verbatim, true, superb – 'My client was highly upset, and so was his dog.'

7 October 2000

AS A TERRIFIC fan of interviews, one of the best I have ever read took place on 15 December 1764, in Switzerland, between those two great men of letters, Boswell and Rousseau. It's true that we would expect their conversation to be lively, quarrelsome, charming. Their lasting contribution to literature is immense: Boswell's *London Journal* and Rousseau's *Confessions* are classic works which have the rare, attractive value of remaining really good to read: in their hands, letter-writing was high art – in 1760, Rousseau wrote this note to Voltaire: 'In short, I hate you.'

Superb. And it's also true that the timing of Boswell's visit to Rousseau was extremely fortunate. Two weeks after Boswell hoofed off, Voltaire wrote a pamphlet which accused Rousseau of abandoning his five children as nameless orphans and killing his mother-in-law by his heartless treatment. He also mentioned in passing that Rousseau suffered from venereal disease. From the moment he read this attack (on 31 December), we are told Rousseau was a broken man, either on the verge of madness or lapsing into complete, raving insanity.

But when Boswell came to his door, Rousseau was happily compos mentis and at the height of his fame. In 1762, he published his main work of political theory, *Le Contrat Social*, with its revolutionary beginning, 'Man is born free and everywhere he is in chains.' Although drummed out of Paris, and then Geneva, he was nicely set up as an exile in Motiers, where he lived more or less as a recluse. His sole income was from writing, and there were no interruptions. Also, he could swan shamelessly around indoors dressed in a loose Armenian kaftan – the poor devil suffered from a constriction of the urethra which caused frequent painful urination.

As for Boswell, he was 24 and in tremendously high spirits, up to his ears in lasciviousness and maliciousness, overjoyed at being made welcome by Rousseau. (But not overwhelmed. 'You have shown me great goodness,' he tells his host, 'but I have deserved it.') They dined in the kitchen. Boswell, a hypochondriac, would have felt quite at home when Rousseau tells him, 'I need a chamber pot every minute.' After scoffing soup, cabbage, turnip, carrots, cold pork, pickled trout, stoned pears and chestnuts, with red and white wines, the two settled down to the serious task of talking a hell of a lot.

Rousseau was clearly charmed by Boswell's rampant ego and roguish manner. Boswell asked him, 'Do you think that I shall make a good barrister before a court of justice?' His answer: 'Yes. But I regret that you have the talents necessary for defending a bad case.'

They discuss literature, class and politics, religion, friendship, women, physiognomy – and cats. It's that particular subject of their interview which I especially adore. From *Boswell on the Grand Tour*, edited by the splendidly named Frederick A. Pottle:

Rousseau: 'Do you like cats?'

Boswell: 'No.'

Rousseau: 'It is my test of character. There you have the despotic nature of men. They do not like cats because the cat is free and will never consent to becoming a slave. He will do nothing to your order, as the other animals do.'

Boswell: 'Nor a hen, either.'

Rousseau: 'A hen would obey your orders if you could make her understand them.'

Priceless. If that was the intellectual tone, unpredictable content and level of retort of modern interviews, I would face *Face the Nation*, tune into *Holmes* at 7pm sharp, listen absorbed to *Morning Report* – 'Nor a hen, either, Prime Minister!' – and would even listen to myself.

A few months ago, I interviewed Ruby Wax. She is an entertainer. She had flown to New Zealand to scare up advance publicity for her stage show, which tours nationwide this week. We met in the bar of some downtown hotel. She wore a tracksuit, no make-up, and very dark glasses. She was short. She drank a glass of water and nibbled at bits and pieces of sushi.

We sat near a window. Dusk was falling, and I watched the light close up shop; on the branch of a tree, a few remaining autumn leaves trembled and shook and seemed desperate to leave.

She rolled her eyes and laughed at a couple of people in the bar – a woman with a nice figure, a guy who had the rasping, dead voice of Billy Bob Thornton in *Switchblade*. These antics seemed to amuse her, absorb her; it was a dreadfully boring interview. I remember absolutely nothing either of us said, except when we had a brief, doomed discussion about literature. Yes, she said, she read widely. 'Just on the off-chance,' I asked, 'have you ever read any of Graham Greene's novels?'

'Naw,' she said. 'I mainly read English authors.'

15 July 2000

LATEST FIGURES state that just over 110,000 New Zealanders are unemployed. Bloody hell. The thought of being on the dole fills me with the worst kind of dread. It reminds me of all the times I used to be unemployed in Wellington, when for something to do I bored myself even more senseless by writing a diary. A sample from my archives . . .

MONDAY

It rained. The only time I left the house was to the dairy across the road for the paper. I wonder if the editor has read my letter of application yet. No interesting news again – not since a former MP was reported to have eaten fish and potato salad in an Auckland prison the other night.

Watched an old film on TV called *Convicts Four*. It had Sammy Davis, who slept with a scarf over his head and said, 'I'm a walking razor blade!'

TUESDAY

[A man's name] gave me $30 to get him some drugs from a mad guy who lives up a mud track in a shack in the bushes. He was lying on a mattress and had the sheets pulled over his beard, but his eyes were wide open, and red, and he gave me a terrible look.

Went out to visit an old flatmate – the last time I saw him he woke everyone up at 6am with cries of, 'I don't want to take my fucking medication!' – at the psychiatric hospital for lunch. He kept repeating he was delighted to see me, and shook my hand several times. He sleeps in a cubicle separated from the rest by a curtain. When we went in for lunch, a Polynesian guy stood at the door and poured the patients a green drink. Lunch was roast beef, a parsnip, a potato and spinach. Quite nice.

WEDNESDAY

Dreamed last night that I was charged with 'ambiguous murder'. [A woman's name] had somehow killed two horses and badly injured a man, but everyone said I was to blame. I was taken from home to the scene of the crime. The street was black, and I could see the shapes of the two horses – black and red horses. I was to spend a week on remand in an Auckland prison.

Bowled along with low hopes to the Post Office loans department. No loan, said the woman. See, she said, look at your last 12 months' history in your savings account – you don't qualify for anything. Take this with you, she said, handing me the sheet of paper that revealed I was not a good loan prospect, and I said thanks, and ripped it into three pieces and put it in the smokers' bin by the door.

Another job interview this afternoon. The editor, a mother of three teenage sons, said at the onset: 'Do you want to work for a community newspaper or are you just desperate for a job?' Doubt if I'll get it.

THURSDAY

Brilliant day. Immersed in thoughts of poverty, I was hunched in front of the one-bar heater this morning when my flatmate came through the door with a letter for me: it contained a Post Office Bank Card. What an amazing thing. I flashed it around town later on in the day. Everyone expressed admiration. I even attempted, with assistance, a go at a Bank Card Machine. Nothing came out, but it was an exhilarating episode.

And then tonight the phone rang, and it was [a woman's name] speaking, saying I love you and I miss you and Darling. She said if I ever travelled to see her it should be a Saturday when her boyfriend plays cricket and is out all day.

FRIDAY

Went into town and bought some comics, and read them next door over coffee at the Hob. This is an old routine of mine which I'll probably continue for the next 600 years.

Another job interview this afternoon. It's in a warehouse, dispatching floral sundries. An old bloke with a bald head who wore an apron conducted the interview. Doubt if I'll get it.

Went to see Unrestful Movements play loudly. Met that guy who was in a car crash a while ago and had brain damage and was not expected to live. A parting in his hair revealed a long shaved patch where a scar had been stitched over. Boring guy, though. Walked [a woman's name] to her house. Apparently her boyfriend has gone to New Plymouth this weekend to sleep in a coffin. We reached the front steps, and she said, 'Do you want to see my bedroom?' We kissed for a few minutes and that was nice but I stupidly went home and it was so cold that I went to bed in all my clothes as well as clutching a hotwater bottle.

SATURDAY

Went to the wharf and sat on the rocks and watched the *Union Hobart* sail in. Highlight of the day.

SUNDAY

Got depressed, so stupidly went to see that homeopath. He took out a pendulum, swung it around, but *he* slipped into a slight trance. Then he gave me bottle of glucose powder and said, 'Expect results!' I set back over the hill and got lost, and had to argue with rock, blackberry and ravine. It rained.

2 December 2000

DIARY OF A PROFESSIONAL NOBODY

HOW VERY, VERY much my character and bearing have changed since I recorded my dismal prospects in the previous column. That diary entry was written sometime in the 1980s. The following is from a week in April 2001.

MONDAY

Fin's away all week because he wants to look after Rosa, so wore a nice white shirt to work to convince myself I am Acting Editor. I like being Acting Editor. I find it very calming to give orders. It makes me a nicer person. And the position brings out tender feelings towards the *Listener*. I think of its 60 years, its fine and noble history, its standards. I think of former editor, the legendary Monte Holcroft, in his cravat. *This is for you, Monte,* I think, as I find a break-out quote for Philip's profile of Henry Rollins: 'What does Rollins make of Limp Bizkit? "It sounds like music for young folks. Every other word is bitch."'

TUESDAY

Jenny came home last night on the train with books bought at Bookstacks – Jessica Mitford's *The Making of a Muckraker,* Don Hadden's *99 New Zealand Birds*, C.H.B. and M. Quennell's *A History of Everyday Things in England*. Handy. She wore her new $499 Kenzo boots I bought her with my first advance from Random House. She looked great. Late night.

Put the magazine to bed at just before one this afternoon. How smooth, how professional. Ordered Karl to get the staff car and drive me downtown to Real Groovy. For my interview with Enya a few weeks ago, I asked her record company to chuck me all her

141

CDs 'for research'. They are all in virgin condition as I trade them in for $62. Think about buying the Coldplay CD for $34.95, but Karl says if I buy a blank CD for $3.95, he'll burn me a copy of the album which he downloaded from Napster. Modern life is brilliant.

WEDNESDAY

Anzac Day. More relevantly, it was soft, beautiful autumn weather, so I sunbathed and dozed for hours in the backyard on my sunlounger. I love that sunlounger. Tim bowled over and we went for one of our aimless drives. Mt Roskill in autumn is particularly aimless. Was going to visit Peter at Mercy Hospital but the nurse said he was asleep. Got back home in time to put on my gumboots and wade across the mudflats at sunset. Presume I saw about 80 pied stilts because the South Island pied oystercatcher isn't called the North Island pied oystercatcher. But it reminded me to hoof up to Westmere and buy eight battered oysters. Scoffed them from the bag as I walked back along West End Road and through the park at dark.

I should waste more time like this.

THURSDAY

A group email from the publisher's PA shakes with rage as she passes on the shocking news that some bastard keeps flicking off the switch of the new fizzy-drinks machine dispenser – three times a day. It will destroy the machine, she warns. 'Who,' I ask Rowan, 'is this fizzybomber?' My guess is that the terrorist is the same person who last week fucked with the controls or something of the office's main computer server. I have a list of suspects, and narrow it down to the two new *Listener* subs or the gay guy at the *Woman's Weekly*.

Whoever the culprit is, it's clear the office is in a state of moral decay, moral torpor, moral despair. The aircon is down, yet again; it was either as cold as the grave today, or hot and arid, the air fetid with the stench of sweat and various odours. The staff bitch and whine and snap. I am unbothered. I am the Acting Editor of the *Listener*. I write headlines – '007's lament', 'No thanks, not hungry', 'When you're dead you get collected' – and edit stories and commission stories and alter designs and choose photos and draw up the next issue and Get On With It, a faux but diligent modern Monte in love with an idea of the *Listener*.

FRIDAY

Busy as hell all day, so grabbed Karl at 10 to five and cabbed it up to the Alhambra. A classic cast list. Russell and Jan behind the bar, Judith at front of house, Rufus and Robbie M onstage, and all the boys out in force by the bar: James D, James W, Jimbo, Bob, Nari, Dixie, Robbie R, Terry, Paul, Doug, and Graeme showed up, and then Tim and Roydon showed up, and Rufus and Robbie played 'You'll Never Walk Alone', and I ordered mushrooms, mussels and meatballs, and hooked into Monteiths Original and . . .

SATURDAY

. . . And woke up not feeling too smart. Got On With It bigtime, though, because Monday is the deadline to complete 10,000 new and original words wanted by Random House to help hawk my book of columns. Thrashed the Coldplay album all day, wandering through to the lounge to turn up 'Yellow', and worked till 4.30am.

SUNDAY

Because there were only about 1,000 words of the book left to write, hoofed up to the bar with Michelle at four this afternoon to hear Bob read his poetry, and there were Russell and Jan behind the bar, and the place was packed, with James D, James W, Jimbo, Nari, Dixie, Terry, Paul, Judith, Connie, Marx, Tracey, David, Olwyn, Tim, Roydon, and Jenny showed up, and then Bob Orr read his poems, and when he did that it was like all the doors of language were open, his words walked right in and did exactly as they pleased, while I sat there, all thumbs on my hamfists, about to write only this.

THE FELLOWSHIP

AFTER AN INTENSE, high-level meeting held in Wellington a few months ago, I can now exclusively reveal that I have won a fellowship to study at Oxford University. I would have been quite happy to be scooped with this news, but I waited, and waited, and nobody else has bothered to report it, even though the *Listener* whipped out a press release which I helped to write. 'While we'll miss him,' editor Finlay Macdonald said with words I put in his mouth, 'it will be good to get him out of the office for a few months.'

I take off sometime in October. The fellowship lasts for three months. They fly you over, put a roof over your head in Green College, give you the run of the place, pay your tuition fees, cough up a weekly stipend, and see you right for 'incidentals and travel within Britain'. They being . . . everyone, by the sound of it. It's a British Chevening David Low Fellowship funded by the British Foreign and Commonwealth Office Chevening Awards Scheme and managed on behalf of the British High Commission in Wellington by the British Council. That's a lot of capital letters, and there are more to come: at Oxford, during the 13-week Michaelmas Term, I will join other overseas journalists on the Reuters Foundation Fellowship Programme. What this all means is that I am really happy.

And apparently I show promise. 'The purpose of the awards,' according to the application form, 'is to allow promising journalists to conduct supervised research into an approved subject relevant to their career.' Applications closed on 13 October last year. My form arrived on 16 October. Bloody couriers. Actually, I think I mailed it. Bloody postal workers. But the woman at the British

Council was very nice, very forgiving. Just as well. I had spent hours composing my proposed study subject, as well as a brief biographical outline ('I attend an exclusive social club most Friday evenings . . .').

A few weeks later, I was told I had made the shortlist and would need to be interviewed by a selection panel at the Wellington offices of the British Council. I rarely consent to give interviews, but decided to make an exception. And so I slipped into a black suit and white shirt, and took a notebook to rehearse the intelligent things I should say at the British Council. The only thing I wrote was one line as the plane passed over Mt Ruapehu. I looked at the notebook again when we landed at Wellington airport. It read, 'Haven't thought of anything yet.'

Inevitably, they couldn't shut me up at the interview. I banged on and blathered, I riffed and rudely interrupted. There was a particularly long, pompous speech about typical qualities in New Zealand writing, which I said were similar to an English, rather than American, sensibility. In what ways? Well, I replied, like the English, New Zealanders tended to be thoughtful, measured, and . . . uh . . . sly. 'Sly?' exploded one of the panel, a woman who was as English as weak tea. She looked like I had just slapped her across the face. Quickly, I blurted, 'A synonym for sly, to my thinking, would be playfulness.' She calmed down, thank God, and I walked unsteadily out after a few more minutes, and straight to a bar where I got as drunk as any number of English lords.

Three nervous weeks later, I got the nod, along with three other journalists. Fantastic. I have since looked up the kind of papers that current Reuters Foundation fellows are studying at Oxford. Bjorn Bredal is surveying the role of newspaper ombudsmen. N. Sriram is researching economic convergence between India and Pakistan. Peter Morgan's paper examines the implications of genetics-based medicine. Ram Narayan Kumar will describe and document human rights abuses, including murder and torture, inflicted against the Sikh population of Punjab.

I will be watching football. More precisely, the approved subject relevant to my career is football journalism. This is my specialist interest. I own 139 football books, from Billy Wright's *The World is My Football Pitch* to *Gazza Agonistes* by poet Ian Hamilton, anthologies featuring football writing by Pinter, Amis, Camus, Borges and Kipling, and it pays to have two copies of the greatest piece of literature ever written, Michael Parkinson's *Best: An Intimate Biography*. But to write about football, you must observe football, and what this means is that I really must go and watch a lot of games of football. Gizzus them incidentals and travel within Britain.

At the end of my term, I'm expected to deliver a lecture. I have some experience in this field. A few years ago, I spoke at a school of journalism and read out a sentence by Brian Glanville, probably the holiest living football writer in England: 'Pele flicked the ball over his head, bounced it whimsically on his thigh, then shot irresistibly past Svensson.' There's one moment in that otherwise boring sentence, I said, which is pure genius, which is startling and impulsive and perfect – the decision to use the word 'whimsically'. No one showed the slightest bit of interest. I think I will make a very good academic at Oxford.

17 March 2001

THE SECOND MAGNUM, THE FOURTH CIGAR

VERY EASILY the best programme over summer has been the repeat series of *Brideshead Revisted*. What lusciousness. Some dates, some names: Evelyn Waugh's 1945 novel was adapted in 1979 by John Mortimer for Granada Television. Generously, the chairman of BBC, George Howard, loaned his rival company the use of Castle Howard for filming. It's the star of the show. It looks absolutely magnificent, and I have lived in it every day for the past few weeks.

Brideshead has played on TV1 each weekday at 12.30pm. Just after the stroke of midday, I have trotted from work to my rented home, fixed lunch, closed the curtains against a harsh New Zealand sun, and sat down to install myself in Castle Howard's opulence and luxury. It has been a rare happiness. Set in the 1920s, *Brideshead* is largely about the friendship between Oxford students Charles Ryder (Jeremy Irons, who narrates) and Lord Sebastian Flyte (Anthony Andrews); when they first meet, and lie beneath oak trees nibbling summer strawberries, and take a langorous holiday together in Venice, Ryder comes up with this amazing lyric: 'I was drowning in honey, stingless.'

Drowning in honey – yes, please. The novel made Waugh rich, but he later gave it a poor review, blaming its excesses on writing in 'a bleak period of soyabeans and black-outs', meaning England during the war. 'In consequence it is infused with a kind of gluttony, for food, and wine, for the splendours of the recent past, and for the rhetorical and ornamental language which now on a full stomach I find distasteful.'

I watched it like a glutton, a fat pig snuffling for more. I loved the 'high insolent dome' of Castle Howard. I loved the stiff clothes and the silver service and the silent butlers and the fireplaces in every room, and I think I especially loved all the booze. Sebastian becomes an alcoholic. As a student at Oxford, Waugh wrote to his friend Tom Driberg: 'Do let me most seriously advise you to take to drink.' Yes, I'll have another, thanks. And another. And then wander past the cedars and the copper beeches in the grounds of Oxford.

The trick is to wander slowly. The series may well be the slowest piece of TV ever made. Nothing happened for so long that I sometimes wondered whether the programme was falling backwards. There was a great scene where Ryder and Sebastian's sister Julia are walking on the deck of the *QE2* towards the rail. It was filmed during a force 8 gale, but the couple, arm in arm, mooched at such a leisurely pace that it seemed the rail was actually getting further away with every step.

I doubt I shall ever be rich. All I got from the latest Bonus Bonds prize draw – I found it in the letterbox on my way home to watch an episode where Julia's fiance buys her a live tortoise with her initials set in diamonds in its shell – was a lousy $20. A shame. It looks so cool to be aristocratic, and dissolute, and deadly charming. 'Charm is the great English blight,' Ryder is warned by Anthony Blanche, an outrageous Oxford homo. 'It spots and kills anything it touches.' Bring it on if you get to talk as brilliantly as that. The series ends with the death of Flyte's father; his Italian mistress says, 'The doctors in Rome gave him less than a year. His heart. Some long word at the heart. He is dying of a long word.'

Fantastic. They don't write TV like that anymore. If ever before. Too bad, though, that a planned film version of *Brideshead* in 1950 fell through – the job of scripting had been offered to Waugh's friend Graham Greene, then at the height of his genius. He would have loved the task. *Brideshead* was his favourite of Waugh's novels, and they were both complete bastards. This is Scobie, from Greene's 1948 novel *The Heart of the Matter*: 'How often he had winced at [his wife's] patronage of strangers. He knew each phrase, each intonation that alienated others.' This is Ryder, from *Brideshead*: 'Throughout our married life, again and again, I had felt my bowels shrivel within me at the things she said.'

I loved Jeremy Irons' dry, tired narration. I met him once. Sort of. I was about to catch the lift in a Sydney hotel room to interview – gosh, she was lovely – Kylie Minogue. The doors opened, I walked in, and there was Irons. He asked in his dry, tired voice, 'What floor?' With a flourish, I announced: 'The top floor, please.' He raised an eyebrow, impeccably, and I shyly studied him in silence. He was tall, thin as a rake and as pale as death – the guy looked like a cadaver. In short, he was still Charles Ryder.

I suppose it's as close as I'll ever get to *Brideshead*. But each day, when the programme finished, I would walk back to work through a park, very slowly, leisurely, at a measured pace, enjoying my afternoon stroll of the grounds of Castle Howard, my ordinary, rental, working New Zealand life further away with each step, even though I was wearing jandals.

27 January 2001

HE LEFT with a glance over his shoulder, the famous eyebrows lifting one last time, and then he was gone. Darkness settled on the TV screen like a full stop. There are still another nine months remaining in our century. But when Brandon Walsh departed *Beverly Hills, 90210* last week, he took the decade – his decade, the '90s – with him.

You bet I cried. It's true that over the past nine years, ever since Brandon showed his wet, do-right face on TV, I have loathed and despised the guy, yelled at him, hooted with derision at his glib responses and girlish reasonings, called him a sook, a pansy, a jackass, and there have been times of such outrage that I dared to consider changing channels. In short, we were close.

It pains me to think that some people have never viewed *90210*, never clasped eyes on Brandon. Here is a brief plot and character summary. It's a compelling melodrama about a group of friends who live in Beverly Hills. Their parents are rich. Their lives, often or at least usually, are hell. Their moral centre has always been Brandon. With his twin sister Brenda, a professional bitch, and his parents Jim and Cindy, actively employed as professional squares, he arrived in LA from Minnesota in our equivalent of his fifth form year at school. From there, he quickly set himself the task of becoming America's answer to Ken Barlow.

Like Ken, he was the most boring man on his continent. How boring? Brandon's friends liked to call him Bran.

Like Ken, he worked as a journalist. Over the years, Bran has crumbled the flakes of his brain in the pages of *The Blaze* (at Beverly

High), *The Condor* (at California University), *Boston Herald* (summer holidays), *Beverly Beat* (after graduating) and, finally, giving actor Jason Priestley the chance to leave *90210*, as the Washington correspondent for the *New York Chronicle*, where he will no doubt emerge as the Christopher Hitchens of his generation.

Like Ken, with dreary Deirdre, he fell for a dillbrain. Bran had Kelly. All that incessant nagging, all those duck-faced whinings! She was very easily brainwashed by the New Evolution cult. She was stalked by a lesbian. She took a lot of cocaine, but didn't enjoy it. A right Little Miss Priss, a Thatcher in a pretty summer dress. And yet Bran stuck to her side, loving, supportive, pussywhipped – like many liberals, he secretly adored the boot in the face.

But he knew right from wrong. Quickly. Two nights on the piss, and he checked into rehab. Sook! In the second season, his girlfriend Emily spiked him with the love-drug U4EA; overjoyed, he humped her on the bonnet of a car outside his beloved milkbar, the Peach Pit. 'This isn't you,' squawked Brenda. The next day, he gave Emily a solemn lecture on choice and responsibility, and broke off the romance. Pansy! After that episode, his only walk on the wild side was his brief, fourth-season decision to grow a goatee. Jackass!

Yes, how I needed him in my life. He was like a warning. Fiction often shows us the Dark Other who resides in the deepest troughs of our mind. It begins in childhood, as we tremble at the unholy appetites of the troll eyeing up those three succulent billygoats. Adult readers tighten their grip on *Crime and Punishment* as Raskolnikov crouches in the darkness and fondles his axe.

Brandon Walsh was drawn in the same primal charcoals. The appalling moral certainties, the stuffed, tucked-in shirt – you could say there is a little bit of Bran inside all of us. But we often envy what we hate. He was terribly handsome. He was voted Most Likely to Succeed at school, and president of the students' association at university. He once delivered a baby in an elevator. When he won $5,000 in a lottery, he gave the money to charity. He was even good at ping-pong.

Unbearable. And impossible to tear myself away. It was an exhausting decade; I have seen his ways, known his face, season after season. No '90s revival will be complete without Bran. He measured the decade, gave it shape and content – he gave it a home.

He was like a classic hit. In the years to come, whenever I think of Bran, vivid images of the '90s will float by – various couches in different flats, the air guitar poses I struck as John E. Davis's bitchin' *90210* tune played, the times in my life when I was happy.

I shall miss him more than I can say. I guess I loved the guy. As he drove away that fateful night, the soundtrack played 'Nightswimming' by Bran's favourite band, REM. Hot tears stabbed at my eyes. Goodbye, old friend. Such a perfect farewell. I've always hated REM.

27 March 1999

MILK, NO SUGAR

YES, AGAIN. Six months have passed since I asked readers to send in their recommendations of good, honest tearooms and coffee lounges, and to help draw up a 'map of New Zealand we can measure in teaspoons . . . Your reports will be gratefully acknowledged.'

Up to January of this year, readers had kindly supplied the names of 36 establishments around the country. 'Thanks for your ongoing cafe guide,' wrote John of Lower Hutt. 'My wife and I have just used it when on a holiday cycling the South Island, and it was invaluable.' Bloody hell. That really was keen. John agreed with earlier recommendations for **Perry's** in Christchurch, the **Lagonda** in Oamaru, **McGregor's** in Palmerston and **Governor's** in Dunedin; adding to the list, he endorsed **Tip Top** in Dunedin's Octagon and the **Manhattan** in Blenheim. Good man.

Stephanie of Ranui raved about **Allie Katz**, on Great North Road, Henderson, praising the scones, the salad sandwiches and even the posters of tulips, which she made sound good enough to eat. Jenny of Napier sent in two photos of the **Paper Mulberry Tree Cafe**, which is apparently a translation of Te Aute – the famous Te Aute College (State Highway 2, 25 minutes from Hastings) is across the road. Ian of Masterton reported on the **Waldorf Tearooms** in Queen Street, Masterton, which enjoys national recognition because Eric, an ex-serviceman, has tucked into a flounder for lunch every day since the end of World War II. Does he still?

A test case for my own tearoom samplings is the quality of the egg sandwich. It ought to be on white bread, no mayonnaise, no parsley, salted, with plenty of the white bit of the egg still alive. Fascinating, but most readers were more alert to sweets. 'Sample the muffins!' exclaimed Fran of Geraldine, writing about the **Plums Cafe** and the **New Riverside Cafe**, both in Talbot Street, Geraldine. 'The best caramel and almond tart in the world,' claimed Diana of Cambridge, of **Fran's Cafe** in her home town. 'Greek lemon cake with yoghurt,' slobbered Margaret, via email, giving two thumbs-up to the **State of the Art Cafe** in Dannevirke: 'We found it en route to hear Kenny Rogers a couple of years ago.' What a brilliant day.

'Have you been told about the excellent tearooms at Patatonga, on state highway 27?' emailed Richard. 'Comfortable lounge area, home cooking and a donkey in the paddock next door.' Hopefully the third attraction is not linked to the second. Other votes came from Ngaire of Te Puke for **Verdini's**, Te Puke; Neville of Merivale for both the **Garden Cafe**, Culverden, and the **Topiary Cafe**, Darfield; Ruth of New Plymouth for **Aromas**, New Plymouth ('I have frequented their coffee lounge for the past 15 years'); and Norma, chairperson of something called Waikanae 2000, typed out a charming note on official letterhead to give praise to the **Bon Appetit**, Waikanae.

A little further afield, Louise of Tokyo – I always knew 'Fool's Paradise' had international appeal – wrote to say how much she missed the **South Pacific Coffee Lounge** in Te Awamutu and the **Chelsea Lounge** in Hamilton. Both have disappeared. Similarly, Jane of Christchurch lamented the overhaul of a formerly 'brilliant little tearoom', **Brigitte's** in Merivale. It used to offer mince on toast, tomato soup and big, fat ham sandwiches. 'It has now become an espresso slophouse where the staff wear T-shirts with the slogan, "There is no 'X' in espresso." What vileness . . .

There are probably hundreds of such tales.'

There are. I have seen it happen many times – the friendly, genuine establishment, open to all, replaced by the preening cafe with insane prices, appalling muck which claims to be food, and an atmosphere that is too frightening, confusing or boring for many New Zealanders, who now have nowhere to sit and relax. It's a disgrace and an affront. 'Please give those espresso machines a fair go!' wrote Margaret, owner of the **Smelting House** espresso slophouse in Greymouth. Nah.

God bless, then, the other places mentioned above, as well as the **Copper Kettle**, Waipara, and the **Home Fresh Bakery**, Barrington Street, Christchurch (both courtesy of Jane of Christchurch). Allow me to declare four votes of my own. I would be nowhere much without **Cafe 300**, a few doors down from the *Listener* offices in Richmond Road, Auckland. A nice woman called Rhonda is in charge. She pours a strong cup of coffee straight from the pot, and makes such an extraordinary salami roll that I recently talked to a girl who drove many miles across town just for that dining pleasure. A shame I had scoffed the last one.

I had the great pleasure of visiting two excellent tearooms recently – the **BB Stop**, Fairlie, and the **Hideaway Cafe**, Stafford Street, Timaru. Both are worthy of national awards. The Hideaway is a whopping big place, carpeted and creamy, at the back of a rather astonishing gift shop, Grandma and Grandpa's Place. As for the BB Stop, it has the terrific advantage of a window table, looking out onto Fairlie's main street.

Finally, on a recent junket to exotic Invercargill, I was bowled over by an almost perfect coffee lounge, the **Sapphire**, in Kelvin Street. There was oyster soup and white bread sandwiches; it had a good view of the street and plenty of tables. But I was especially bowled over by the sight of an antique espresso machine, a La

Cimbali, and the only source of coffee on the premises.

What gives, I asked May, the friendly proprietress. She then told me a nice story. The Sapphire, she said, was Invercargill's first coffee lounge. It was built 48 years ago by a local man who had been in the air fleet during World War II. When he returned home, he brought back a French-Canadian war bride. It was on her wishes that the La Cimbali was imported from Milan. They sold the Sapphire in about 1971, and still live in the area.

There was something moving about this exotic little narrative; it was like a romance novel, and you could imagine the star-crossed couple sitting down at the end of the book to eat a buttered scone. Heaven knows what other geographies of love exist in the tearooms and coffee lounges of the nation. I should love to find out courtesy of correspondents. On your bike, John and John's wife of Lower Hutt.

17 June 2000

THIS IS THE best sports column in New Zealand. You have it on good authority from the Hillary Commission National Sports Journalism Awards 2000, held in Wairakei last Sunday night, when I stepped up onstage to shake cabinet minister Trevor Mallard's hand and accept the Spalding Award for Best Columnist. Fantastic. Me happy. And what a tremendous weekend. I got drunk as 40 bastards, ate lots of meat, enjoyed the hospitality of the Wairakei Resort for twice as long as I had expected, met legends and some interesting birds, and can now look forward to never being offered any kind of position in the governmental offices of Trevor Mallard.

The weekend began as it finished. I woke up drunk. A Friday night on the sauce at the Alhambra will do that. But I manfully staggered out of bed at 8.14am, showered, packed a suitcase, kissed my wife goodbye and hoofed it to the bus station at 9am for the five-hour ride to Wairakei.

It was a dreary day, wet and foul, as I guzzled tea from my thermos and blearily gazed at the dim Saturday countryside until the bus dropped me off outside the hotel. I had made excellent time. In fact, it turned out I had arrived a day early: the awards night was on Sunday. Yes. You could say I felt like a goose. Reception staff led me to Hillary Commission wallahs, who were busy doing up the stage; superbly, they decided to shout me a room for the two nights, after I found out I could catch a bus back home at two in the morning on Sunday, arriving Auckland at 6.50am, ready to resume my job as the *Listener*'s Acting Editor.

What to do alone in a hotel in the middle of pine forest nowhere?

Doze. Swim about a dozen laps – yes, entire widths – in the heated pool. Look at people playing golf and wonder why they do it. Gnaw on room service steak. Watch football on TV. Stand by State Highway 1 at night and watch, trembling, as vast, fulminating petrol and logging trucks roar past. Doze . . . It was all very pleasant, except when I went for a walk on Sunday afternoon along the side road beside Wairakei's famous geothermal power plant; at a bend, facing enormous gusts of steam that obscured oncoming tour buses, I thought it best to perhaps turn back, and was convinced of this action when a lovely, white, yellow-beaked bird came out of nowhere and flew straight at my head. I fended the bastard off with my umbrella, and continued to do so as it made repeated attacks while I hot-footed my way back to the hotel.

Bring on the awards night. Loved it. To a man, and Mary Durham from TV1, sports writers are a great crowd. Hearty, solid, smart, they are generous souls, and are usually the best reads (Marc Hinton, *Sunday Star-Times*; Chris Rattue, *New Zealand Herald*) in their newspapers. I hooked up with my chum Gordon Brown of the *Daily News* in New Plymouth, who introduced me to legends (Alex Veysey, D.J. Cameron), and then insisted I join the Taranaki mafia at his table, where I gnawed on a rack of lamb. By that time, I was a celebrated gnawer: genial host Keith Quinn had announced from the stage that I was sports columnist of the year.

Contestants are required to choose three selections from the past 12 months. Good one. In that time, I have written exactly three columns that refer to sport. One about the scrapbooks I kept as a kid on George Best, one about the joys of playing mini-golf, and one about a sex and drugs scandal involving Mark Todd's horse. There you have it. Blame the judge. His name is Bob South. I have no idea who he is, but I love him. From his judging remarks: 'Braunias's irreverence is both explicit and commendable.' Cheers,

Bob, but I'm sure the word you were looking for was 'irrelevance'.

After dinner, sports minister Trevor Mallard got up and spoke for 27 years. I left after three or four, met a top bloke from TVNZ and cartoonist Garrick Tremain, and that's when I really got stuck into the piss – Garrick is a great old geezer, and somehow his louche manner makes you want to knock back whatever's going.

Mallard's droning ballad finally came to an end. A couple of people approached me and filled my head with a number of scurrilous things he had apparently said about me on stage. Athletically, I jumped to my feet, found his table and laid into the poor devil. It really was a shocking performance. Sample roaring quote: 'I voted for your lot, you fuckwit, and this is what I get . . . You disgust me!' (Actually, I had never heard of him until that night.) He asked for specific reasons. This made me even more livid; after ignoring several hands being laid on my shoulder to drag me away, I stomped off, resumed my happy behaviour, laughed, blathered, drank more, somehow remembered to pack, and was escorted by two blokes – possibly hotel security – across the highway to the 24-hour gas station where I climbed on the 2am bus to Auckland and immediately fell into a coma.

The prize for winning, by the way, is $1,000 worth of golf equipment.

18 November 2000

FOR SALE

FOR SALE: some really nice golf stuff. There is a lightweight carrybag containing a complete set of nine Spalding clubs, which are fit to grace any course in the world. Apart from the putter, long and lean with its stainless steel shaft, the woods and irons are all adorned with graphite shafts. Shafts are good. Shafts do the business. As well, there is a box of 10 golf balls, made by the famous Chicopee, Massachusetts, golfing brand Top-Flite, whose appealing registered trademark is 'The Longest Balls'. We all know long balls also do good business.

The whole brand-new lot is up for grabs. In an exclusive 'Fool's Paradise' offer, they could be yours – for a price, and a for a good cause.

Regular readers – all 17 lost souls – may recall that last week's column bragged on about how I was recently judged sports columnist of the year at the Hillary Commission National Sports Journalism Awards. The prize was $1,000 worth of golf equipment. Gleaming, handsome, as pure and virgin as untrod snow. Yes.

Spalding Sports sponsored the award. I picked up the prize at their premises last week, where I met a quietly spoken woman with attractive shoes, a bright-eyed bloke who wore a red shirt, and an older guy who runs the place. Because sports columnists of the year are by nature men of few words, and because I got the feeling no one believed who I said I was, I blurted, 'Thanks very much!' and ran for it, bundling the prize into the back seat of *Listener* photographer Jane Ussher's car. Ever since, the bag with its clubs and long balls has sat in the magazine's reception, and driven most visitors and our advertising guy Jason Sharma mad with envy.

But what do I want with golf gear? It's true that I have a certain affection for the sport, dating back to one Wellington winter when I earned a few coins as a golf correspondent for a Sunday newspaper – I would catch a train to some suburban station, trudge off to the golf course and spend an extremely pleasant afternoon chatting to golfers about anything they cared to say that would help round out my terse 200-word reports phoned in back at the clubhouse. How well I remember the smell of pine trees, the fresh air and vast skies and tender sunsets, the profound, disturbing melancholy of being 23 years old and standing in a fairway in the rain. I have absolutely no memory of golf.

Some of my best friends are golfers. I'll occasionally watch golf on TV and feel soothed by the green screen. I once went on a junket to Queenstown and had a grand old time learning how to drive a golfcart at some fancy golf course. I really like playing mini-golf. What I'm getting at is that I have absolutely no interest in golf.

Which is why I'm taking the opportunity to use this column to hawk off the golf equipment – with all proceeds going to charity. The rules are simple. Make a generous offer. Don't be stingy, or bore me to tears by pledging something comical like $5 – in fact, I will not accept anything beneath $700. Nominate the charity of your own choice. The highest bidder will be contacted and asked to write a cheque made out to the registered organisation concerned. Post to me at the *Listener* address. I will arrange its transfer and confirm that the cheque has been cleared – apologies for the mistrust, but this country is full of rogues – before contacting the winner to sort out delivery of the golfing gear. Fair enough?

Sorry if the price is too steep. But it's still a bargain. Remember, the stuff is worth $1,000: is brand new, gleaming, handsome, untouched, etc: and is also a lot more use than the usual nonsense offered at so-called celebrity auctions. Think of those graphite shafts, those long balls. Think of the good that your money will bring when you give it to those in need. Christmas is just around the corner. Foodbanks, refuges, shelters. The poor, the beaten, the mad. Half-starved cats, anxious whales. Whatever. You know the score.

Many readers are probably up to their ears in debt, fretting about the phone bill, dying for their next drink. Join the club. But some of you – yes, yes, this is the *Listener*, not the *National Business Review* – must be able to stump up the cash, or must know someone with a well-hung wallet, an eye for a tee, a desire to help.

A few weeks ago, I invited readers to send in the names of good second-hand bookstores around the county. The response has been huge. I rather doubt my golf-for-charity scheme will attract a similar number of offers. Failure to attract any willing participants will be dealt with as expected: I'll keep quiet about the matter, place a for-sale ad in the newspaper and pocket the cash. Charity – you have no doubt been expecting this pithy sentiment – begins at home.

25 November 2000

GIVE

IN WHICH THE winner can now be announced of this column's recent charity auction. A few weeks ago, I gave notice that readers could bid for a lovely set of golf stuff – lightweight carrybag, clubs and balls, all brand new and worth $1,000 – which the nice people at Spalding Sports chucked at me as first prize for picking up a rather unlikely sports writing award. The rules were simple. Bids would not be accepted under $700, and readers could nominate their own charity. As well, I would make absolutely sure that the highest bid was in good faith.

It's true that a mean, grasping side of me hoped that no one would apply, so that I could simply hawk off the golf gear in private and pocket the cash. Too right I could do with the money. A couple of days after the offer was published, I toddled off to an ATM machine and read the four worst words in the English language: TRANSACTION DENIED. INSUFFICIENT FUNDS.

Well, I'll manage. I probably earn more than you. But what about those in much greater need? There were eight offers for the golf stuff. Seven were serious. One bid was much higher than the rest. In which the winner . . . cannot really be announced, because he asked to remain anonymous, but I doubt he'll mind if I refer to him as Robin of Wellington. His cheque has been banked, and cleared, and the amount is for $2,000.

Cheers, Robin. You're a bloody good man. His two grand has gone to the Downtown Community Ministry of Wellington. I gave director Kevin Hackwell a bell, and he told me that Robin had requested his money go to the ministry's foodbank – on average,

Kevin reckons, 1,500 parcels are handed out over the year, but that demand is always higher before Christmas. He estimates 50 parcels a day at the moment.

As well, there is a programme which administers the finances of itinerants – apparently, they tend to migrate south in the summer and to Auckland in winter, usually on the run from debts. The ministry also works as an advocate for beneficiaries. Kevin claims between a third and a half of welfare dependants are not getting their proper entitlement: 'There are some good people working at Winz, but in general, the corporate culture of Winz is atrocious . . . We're quite a political group.' His own background is in science. Why does he do what he does now? 'Because,' he says, 'people need it.'

Well said. And sincere thanks to everyone else who wanted to help meet other needs. Steve via email offered $1,100 to the charity of my own choice. Ron of Dunedin wished to forward $1,020 to the Salvation Army, which was also the preferred charity of a Whakatane man who asked for anonymity and came up with the precise sum of $1013 – on account of the fact he wanted to give the golf clubs to his 13-year-old son. Marina of Auckland wrote to say she was a mum at home with two young children, and the most she could offer was $300 to the SPCA in Mangere, where she works as a volunteer: 'I would donate the clubs back to them . . . They are having a gala day called Woofstock early next year and they always have a charity auction and the clubs could be sold again.'

A lovely idea. Mike had similar plans. His email began, 'Steve, I've just jumped on my trusty Big Buffalo and cycled through the streets of Tokyo to come to the nearest Internet cafe on this chilly November night after reading your latest instalment in my freshly delivered *Listener* . . . The charity of my and my wife's choice is the refugees of Miyale-jima.' He explained a volcano exploded on the island a couple of months ago and devastated the local population. But if his $1,001 offer was successful, he said, he had no need for the golf clubs – instead, he wanted me to put the gear up for auction in another column.

An anonymous gentleman of Auckland sent a terrifyingly formal letter – he must be a lawyer – offering $1,050, dividing into three $350 lots for social organisations Te Rakau Hua O Te Wao Tapu in Wellington, Sisters of Mercy in Wiri, and the Te Whanau Tuhunotia Trust in Manukau City, which administers the Northern Residential Centre in Manurewa for at-risk children and teenagers. Residents recently performed a Jim Moriarty play at the centre; the production is also staged at the New Zealand Drama School in Wellington from 14–20 December.

Finally, there was a long and probably heartfelt letter from Peter, a 'low-income golfing nut and weekend alcoholic' of Rotorua, who noted my 'otherwise totally ignored column', worked out his weekly booze allowance (three dozen cans at $11.25 each, one $8.50 vodka refill) and accordingly offered $42.25. Merry Christmas, Peter, and by all means take your head out of your ass.

The selfish and the wise love to blather on about how mere charity cannot solve the appalling inequities of the world. Quite right. As such, it may or may not be appropriate that I am planning to deliver the clubs to Robin in Wellington by driving from Auckland with a chum – a Communist who owns a Rolls Royce.

23 December 2000

DO NOT BUY THIS GIFT

THERE ARE plenty of other Christmas presents. Food. Drink. Money. Something simple, something that works. The last thing you want is to buy a gift that baffles, that bamboozles, that brings the receiver one step further towards despair. Do not buy the Lucky Cat.

I was given it recently as a housewarming present. 'You shouldn't have,' I told Diana, and events were to prove I was right on the money. Apparently it's a traditional Japanese symbol of prosperity and good fortune. In brackets, it says, 'Maneki Neko', which translated means Lucky Cat.

The packaging – by Nuvo Accessories, 10 West 33rd Street, New York, NY 1001 – declared that my present was inflatable. Nuvo's pithy advertising line blathered, 'When cool looking furniture is just a breath away!' Well, even my best friends congratulate me for being full of wind, so I opened the box and plucked out the Lucky Cat.

It came with instructions. I like instructions. Language becomes an arithmetic (steps, procedures, everything in its right place), and I really like arithmetic – whenever someone at the office begins boring me to tears, I fill my head with sums, divisions and assorted basic equations. Even so, I doubted that I needed instructions before pursing my lips against the Lucky Cat.

'Warning,' the instructions began, giving me pause. 'Do not over inflate. Please read these instruction before use.' Please add plurals before writing instructions, I would have thought, but I read on. 'This product is not intended for use by children under 3. Adult supervision is required at all times. Product should be check for any loose or broken parts and discarded.' I swept the house for tots, then checked for broken parts. Neither was in evidence. The future looked bright for the Lucky Cat.

Then the small print laid it on thick. 'Do not over inflate,' it repeated. 'Do not try to remove every last wrinkle. This will cause over inflation. Do not use a high pressure hose to inflate.' Oh, come on. Did they really even suspect that was any way to treat the Lucky Cat?

Yes, they did. 'If compressor or pump is used, inflate only 80% and finish inflation by mouth.' What nonsense. But then: 'Those suffering from asthma, bronchitis, heart disease, high blood pressure or any breathing or physical difficulties, should not inflate this product by mouth. If dizziness or nervousness occurs when inflating this product, stop and rest then consult your doctor.'

Any physical difficulties. Bloody hell. Nervousness had most certainly already occurred, but it was a Sunday and where would I find a doctor? Was I really up to the job? When did I last have a medical? Convinced my whole life that I would be the kind of sap who dies in pathetic circumstances – walked into a traffic light, walked beneath a falling piano – it now seemed possible that I might expire while inflating the Lucky Cat.

But even if I survived that first time, what then? Page two of the instructions was headlined, 'Maintenance and deflating'. It ranted, 'The air inside your product is subject to atmospheric changes, such as gravity, temperature and barometric pressures. For example, oxygen mixed with carbon dioxide tends to move from a high pressure area to a low pressure area through a process called osmosis. Therefore, your product should be refreshed with more air once to twice a week.'

Fahgeddit. It sounded like a suicide mission – or like Russian roulette, except the cartridges might be loaded with a sudden, hidden form of physical difficulty. *A man died quite absurdly yesterday, guffawing mourners say. He breathed his last while trying to give life to the Lucky Cat.*

There were so many other complexities. Where to put the blasted thing? 'Keep away from heat. Heat will cause over inflation. Cold will cause contraction . . . In cold areas products should be submerged in warm water before inflation to reduce stiffness.' Is that stiffness in the breather or the Lucky Cat?

'These products are designed with a support column air compression system,' it continued. 'They use an "I" beam construction that distributes the air into several pockets. The suggested weight guidelines are, chairs: 180–200lbs, sofas: 360–400lbs, ottomans: 100–130lbs.' Have you weighed *your* ottoman recently? 'Caution should be used when reaching the suggested weights.' What the hell does that mean? But the instructions seemed to favour the use of a chair: 'For best stability, chair should be placed against a supporting wall.' Otherwise, I suppose, the chair might topple to the ground and annihilate that goddamned Lucky Cat.

Daredevils may feel challenged to go out and buy it at once. Others might have a sudden urge to punish easily worried friends and relatives by giving it to them as a Christmas present. Please, don't. Christmas is a time for spreading joy, for being real nice to people. It is not a time for complicating matters by presenting anyone with the traditional Japanese symbol of good fortune and prosperity, the Lucky Cat.

18 December 1999

AS WE APPROACH the new lunar year, right now is a good time to state that I used to write the astrology page for *Metro* magazine. I was very good at it. Apologies if the claim seems immodest. But the fact is that I have a gift for reading the stars. Ask the staff at the Royal NZ Astrology Institute. They have often consulted me for advice. All of which is meant to back my claim that what you are about to read is the only horoscope for the following year that you'll need.

Capricorn (23 Dec–20 Jan)

You really can be infuriating, with your hot flesh, your violent distemper, your strictly enforced privacy laws. Good for you. Hell is other people. Next year should be a smooth ride as long as you stick to your guns. But it's also important to attend to matters of personal hygiene. Please, bathe often. Only the mind should remain filthy. Happy birthday!

Aquarius (21 Jan–19 Feb)

The dawning of your age has come and gone, and what do you have to show for it? Life has seemed like a dour 0–0 draw. Nobody is cheering from the sidelines. It's time to move on from any great expectations. Seek comfort, agreeable company, bland reassurance. Do community work, and by all means take out a subscription to *North & South*.

Pisces (20 Feb–20 March)

Something smells fishy, and it's probably you. All those dirty little secrets are about to come home to roost. Travel looks inevitable. Are you ready? Start a fitness regime, and cut back on frivolous spending. Make sure all that hard work over the past 12 months doesn't go to waste. Heartlessness can be its own reward.

Aries (21 March–20 April)

You would like to perform random acts of violence. Fair enough. Everyone's got it in for you, and that sound you hear at 3am is work colleagues sharpening their really long knives. Get in first. Drink more and if you see food, eat it. Encourage your delusions. You can always plead insanity afterwards. It might be best to avoid your parents.

Taurus (21 April–21 May)

The fact you may never have had an original thought in your life should play to your advantage. Follow orders, go with the flow, talk in slogans, listen to talkback, attend stand-up comedy shows, live in shadows, and just you watch as your career goes from strength to strength. Remember: it's not about you, it's about all of us.

Gemini (22 May–21 June)

You're a sensitive soul, sentimental and easily misled, a quivering wreck when it gets too hot in the kitchen, a swaggering braggart when things go your way, amusing in small doses, intellectually second division, two faced, double what you're worth, at once saintly and a selfish swine, sleepless, nervous, perverse, prone to fantasies, full of profound longings, and you drink too much. Same again this year.

Cancer (22 June–23 July)

Maturity is a vice. This looks like your year of living dangerously – sexual misconduct gets bad press, but don't believe everything you read. Acting out your own shallow and puerile bedroom farce with complete strangers night after night should be the exactly the kind of liberating experience you have always craved. Disgust yourself. Exceed recommended drug levels, and see your family doctor.

Leo (24 July–23 Aug)

Stop obsessing about work. Office politics is the most tedious game in town. The good news is that you look set for a long trip to foreign lands later in the year – a place where people will begin to notice you and appreciate your loveliness and your intelligence. About time. You really have so much going for you. When's dinner?

Virgo (24 Aug–23 Sept)

Why are people afraid of you? Who cares? It's true that you get as angry as a bear with a sore head, express flatulent opinions as if they were the word of God, and demand, demand, demand – but that's not your problem. Keep it up. No one's perfect. We all have different energy levels. It might be best to avoid having children.

Libra (24 Sept–23 Oct)

You're the top story in your own news hour this year. It should only take four or five pithy sentences to describe – and the key words are likely to be birth and shopping. Good one. Eat your greens, and get plenty of rest. March through to August is a good time to hibernate. Don't forget your friends.

Scorpio (24 Oct–22 Nov)

Do you know any jokes? You'll need a good laugh this year – the key word is crisis. The mere act of walking across the street will cause upheavals and create the kind of drama you thought belonged in nightmares. Wake up and smell the coffee. Stay alert at all times. Did you really expect to get away with it for ever? See your family lawyer.

Sagittarius (23 Nov–22 Dec)

It's crucial that you start off on the right foot this summer. The issue at stake is your physical appearance, because the harsh fact of the matter is that no one is remotely interested in your mind. People can be such bastards. Join the club. Become everything you despise, even if it kills you. Remember: losing is for losers.

6 January 2001

Man wet

A man went for a swim yesterday in the surf at Whangamata. Onlookers described the weather as 'warm'. Clad only in togs, the man stood up from where he had been lying on a beachtowel, and raced down the beach and into the water. 'It was wet,' he said.

Man and woman have sex

A reliable source claims that a Maori woman who appears on television had sex with her husband last night, prompting speculation that the woman might have a bun in the oven and give birth to a child in nine months' time. 'I hurt my foot crouching outside their bedroom window,' said the source, who added: 'Local iwi should be consulted.'

Bloody hell

Brown, a 77-year-old Dargaville man, said he lay on top of the widow up to five times in an attempt to gain an erection but failed and in the end gave up when he fell to the floor. He told the court, 'I didn't get an erection, so I thought, "What's the use?"'

Nice day for it

There were 53 hours of sunshine recorded in the North Island yesterday.

Nice for some

John Hawkesby was seen on the street yesterday. 'Morning,' he said.

Climber falls

An Australian narrowly escaped death when he fell 40m in Mt Cook National Park yesterday. Stephen Graham, aged 36, was recovering in hospital last night from head and abdominal injuries. Constable Mark Stephens, of Twizel, said that if Mr Graham had fallen a further 20m he would have slipped over a cliff and been killed.

Man dead

A man died yesterday.

Good Knight

Sir Bufton Tufton, named in the New Year's Honours List for services to cost cutting, said he expected some ribbing from colleagues when he returns to work. 'I'll have the last laugh when I make them redundant,' he joked. He added that he expected colleagues would still call him 'sir'.

Local iwi consulted

Wellington man Local Iwi, 33, was consulted yesterday.

Doesn't know

A number of people are concerned that fireworks left over from New Year's Eve celebrations might ignite if either kept next to a stove or lit with a match. 'I don't know what the world's coming to,' said Marjorie Stiles, 93, of Westport. 'There weren't any fireworks in my day. Apart from crackers and sky rockets. Oh, they were marvellous! Not like now. Everything's so expensive. I don't know. I really don't.'

Curtains for the Big Man

Jonah Lomu wants to buy some curtains for his new home, according to reports. 'They'll look good against the windows,' the All Black, or someone who certainly resembled the All Black, was overheard to remark on a public footpath the other day.

Story from an Australian newspaper

A Darwin man told yesterday how his left arm was amputated after being bitten nine times by a deadly snake. Gordon Lyons said he was bitten by the snake, considered to be one of the most venomous, after he picked it up from the side of the road. He admitted he was drunk at the time. He said, 'I remember the guys at the Mandarah Pub wanted something to put in their fish tank. But I made the stupid mistake of grabbing it with my left hand because I was holding a beer in my right hand . . . Its fangs were so big that it ripped my hand open. I tore it off me and put it in a plastic bag and threw it in the back of the car. For some stupid reason., I stuck my hand back in the bag, and it bit me another eight times.' Mr Lyons said he began vomiting and suffering diarrhoea about three seconds later. He said, 'My mate was trying to keep me awake by whacking me in the head and pouring beer on me.'

Story from a New Zealand newspaper

Otaihau woman Tania Baker has won a $3,500 dishwasher, dryer, washing machine and fridge freezer in a special promotion put on by Bernie McGinty, the manager of Kaikohe New World. 'It's really funny,' said Tania, 'because my friend dreamed she was going to win the draw. Then my name came out.'

Boats wet

Yachts raced in the America's Cup yesterday. Onlookers described the weather as 'warm'. Watching TV coverage from his home in Ashburton, a man who declined to be named said there were two boats in the water. 'They got wet,' he said.

22 January 2000

SUMMER

YES, THIS IS IT, this is New Zealand – open, and dazed, and you have sand in your hair and sand in your pockets, and every day is like Sunday. The sunsets are shocking pink, outrageous, would you look at that. The air in front of you is wrinkled with heat. Mt Ruapehu is as bald as a coot, Lake Tekapo needs a drink. You are walking on hard, pale clay. There are monarch butterflies, and cicadas, and moths, and flies, mosquitoes, wasps, ants, and visiting aunts.

We are summer islands – the beach, the dust, the light. It suits us. It *makes* us. It's the way we imagine ourselves, and brag about it to the rest of the world. Postcards from Taupo, Nelson, even Greymouth, and 'Wish you were here.' Some of our best literature has suntan lotion on its pages – Sargeson's *That Summer*, Duggan's *Along Rideout Road*, Frame's *The Reservoir*, and if you close your eyes while reading Stead's *All Visitors Ashore* you see orchards and wharves, bare legs and open windows.

It's our time. A national dress is established: we go outdoors wearing the kind of clothes that make us look like hicks. Summer has a New Zealand brand: L&P, Tip-Top, Huttons. We know what to expect. TV plays rubbish. Some bore gets awarded a knighthood. Shell Cup Cricket. Road tolls. Sex, hopefully. The tent, the garden hose.

Optimists will blandly claim it's always good to be alive, but summer most definitely has advantages. Food tastes better. You're insane if you think anything beats sliced cucumber and radishes in a bowl of vinegar with lots of salt at the ready. Even vegetarians stop looking so miserable, although it's true one of the most pitiful sights of the modern age is a vegetarian at a barbecue. Steak. Sausages. Chops. Chooks. Shish kebabs. Burgers. Prawns. Fish. And by all means try barbecued Wattie's fish fingers. Fantastic.

Your gob, your stomach, your entire flesh. Skin smells and tastes delicious in the sun. No doubt many will spend summer on top of jetskis and racing bikes, up and down mountains, and in and out of various beds. Good for them. But this is also the best time to perform that most vital bodily function – sleep. It's nice to doze while the morning ripens like a big fat fruit. A nap is a splendid way to ignore the screeching afternoon. As for evenings – yes, too right the thing to do is have another good, long snizz, and it doesn't get better than if a sulking night finally bursts into a thunderstorm, with the wind lunging at your bedroom curtains through the open window, and the rain steaming off the ground by morning.

Summer demands that you hang a sign over your brain: *Back in 5 minutes*. So you sleep, and you eat, and what's left of your mind is boggled by heat. The cat is as weak as a kitten. You could fry an egg on the pavement. There is so much yellow defeating the earth – gorse, broom, buttercup, lupin. Summer is powerless, exposed. Nothing is as it was. Unplugged and unwanted, schools become ghost towns – the chairs on desks, the dark rooms, the complete silence of the playground as you bend over to drink from an outside basin tap. Sports day, the history exam – their terrors shrivel up and die.

Offices, too, are revealed as nothing more than flimsy walls and the kind of footsore carpets that you wouldn't let your dog vomit on. All work is a sham and summer knows this for a fact, laughs in its face.

The trampoline, the icetray. We are freed from the shocking political event. Old people play cards on folding chairs in their caravans at night. Kids run a lot. There are books to read, and heaven knows what they call that kind of music these days to be played until dawn at nightclubs. Loneliness will cut like a really big knife. Nothing happens so much that the newspapers are driven to publishing stories about buskers.

All summers are endless, sloppy, childish. But the fact that this is the first summer of the new millennium might sharpen our act – the unknown future ripe with promise. The next century is like Robinson Crusoe's desert island: those first footsteps on the sand are ours, it's up to us to reshape the world as we see fit. In short, this is the time for all sorts of lunatic ideas.

Fair enough. Look at those perfect, virgin numerals on the calendar: the year 2000. Anything could happen. These are exciting times. But the days just get on with it – the willow dangling in the slow creek, the flame-grilled feeling of the fish finger – blue and lovely and shimmering.

1 January 2000

MILK, NO SUGAR

THERE IS A postcard I like. It has lamingtons in it – gigantic lamingtons, falling off the Nape Nape Cliffs in Canterbury into the sea, and the artist is the brilliant Ashley W. Smith. I snapped it up recently, and it immediately reminded me that it was high time this column once more got around to yet another instalment in its celebration of good, honest New Zealand tearooms and coffee lounges, where coffee is poured straight from the pot, egg sandwiches await the gentle squeeze of tongs, and the happy existence of lamingtons tells you so much that is fine and decent about this country.

My latest update has to record the devastating news I heard about back in October, when Martin of Raumati South sent me a report by journalist Steve Rendle in the *Evening Post*: 'Friday was a black day for fans of old-fashioned coffee and a good honest feed – Willis St lost its last oasis in the encroaching desert of long blacks, short blacks, flat whites, and strange variations on quiche. After more than 33 years in the business, the Pioneer Coffee Lounge closed its doors. It served both kinds of coffee – black and white – and pies, sausage rolls, asparagus rolls in white bread, lamingtons, and the best raspberry squares around.'

Martin attached a note, headed, 'Another one bites the dust.' Not just another one. This was pretty much my favourite tearoom in either island. I loved it there. I kissed there and dreamed there and sat there for hours. I always took a seat by the front window. It was dark, and quiet, and it had a soft carpet. It was the best.

Still, I'm glad that it at least got a fond send-off in the *Post*, and

I have to admit I wasn't altogether unsurprised at its demise. A bloke who phoned me around about June said that he was probably going to buy the place and do it up. I said that I didn't like the sound of that. He claimed he would keep some of its character. I asked whether that just meant he was planning to design an espresso slophouse. He ummed and ahhed and I never heard from him again and I do not particularly want to.

More immediately, **Cafe 300**, a few glad steps from the *Listener* offices, closed down just before Christmas, and has made work an even more bland and uncouth affair. Any magazine publisher with a nearby tearoom and who wishes to hire my services can call now.

Apologies for the bitter tone. But it's true that coffee lounges are disappearing all over the shop. Linzi of Wellington sent me a column from *Contact* newspaper, headlined TRIBUTE TO A DYING ICON, in which Emily Symons also lamented the passing of the Pioneer, and the great Matterhorn in Cuba Street, although I was relieved to read that the **Crystal Lake Coffee Lounge** in Manners Mall is still alive and brewing.

Espresso slophouses continue to barge in with their foreign muck and their bad manners. Peter of Westport posted a story from the *Coaster* newspaper, which quoted the owner of Greymouth's Smelting House Cafe: 'New Zealanders outside of the Coast can see that we are quite cosmopolitan, not some backward generation whose cafes only serve cream buns.' Jane of Christchurch sent me a *Press* article about former tearoom Brigittes Espresso Bar in Merivale. 'It has always been a timeless and traditional cafe,' blathered the proprietress. Jane acidly wrote in a nice blue felt pen: 'Used to be.'

Meanwhile, Anna of Auckland has written to me, outlining her plans to photograph a book of New Zealand tearooms, 'an important part of our heritage that is slowly starting to disappear'. I trust

Creative New Zealand will slip Anna a handsome grant for her funding application.

But the heritage still has legs. 'I'm a bit loath to reveal this hidden treasure,' emailed A.G., referring to the vast, cheap, superb second-floor cafe in **St Lukes**, Auckland. Anna and Tessa emailed to wax lyrical about the tearooms in **Pleasant Point** ('People detour to get there') and the **Savoy** in Waimate: 'Here the 1950s have truly been preserved, from the orange juice machine to the aluminium milkshake cups to the starched, forest-green of the staff.' Pip, also by email, recommended the **Sponge Kitchen** in Levin, while Mary's email pointed to that balmy town's **Country Lady Cafe**. A shame Levin doesn't support a magazine industry.

My own travels over recent months have led me to a number of top establishments. In the North Island, there is the **Red Rose Cafe** in Te Puke, the **Timber Museum and Tearooms** in Putararu, the fabulous **Crystal Bar Tearooms** in Taihape, and the extraordinary **Skyliner Tearooms** in Brynderwen. 'This business and property is proudly owned by Norman and Sharron Dalebrook and family,' reads a big sign, and that pride is justified in their legendary $5 mountain of bacon and eggs. Most incredibly, a large mural of the sea and the bush surrounds the cafe, and obscures a spanking view of . . . the sea and the bush. Go there at once.

A few days after I snapped up Smith's lamingtons postcard, I found myself in the **ABC Quick Lunch Cafe** in Tainui Street, Greymouth, wolfing down a whitebait sandwich for $5.50. Fantastic. Stayed there nearly an hour. Had absolutely no desire to ruin my holiday by dining anywhere 'quite cosmopolitan'.

13 January 2001

THE TRUTH ABOUT MILK,
NO SUGAR

I would
take him
to a tearoom
in a two story town
that serves
white bread with
mustard & ham
4 & 20 pies
in thin
paper
  bags.
 – Bob Orr

HOPE YOU LIKE the cover. Obviously I married a genius – look at that beautiful composition of object and space, the feminine blue and the shocking pink, the casual yet artful crumple of the white paper bag. Yes, Jenny has done a lovely design job, but there is no escaping the fact that what you are looking at is a lamington. It was an easy choice. There are five columns in this book devoted to the subject of good, honest New Zealand tearooms and coffee lounges. You could pull gently on the bow and say they act as a theme for the book, with its feeling for the small and apparently insignificant, its loathing of anything corporate or pompous. Reviewers are welcome to do so.

As they originally appeared in the *Listener*, each column was intended as a kind of campaign on behalf of tearooms, a celebration, a call to honour and keep them on the landscape. All that the accumulated columns have probably achieved – and the lamington basking so lusciously and temptingly on the book's cover only adds to it – is to turn my good, honest intention into a fetish, a quirk, a vaguely amusing quaintness.

My fault. The columns are too passive, too odd. In any case, the campaign was always going to be a losing battle against the surging, stinking tide of the espresso slophouse, which has continued to wash away tearooms and coffee lounges. Let them eat focaccia. But the truth about my 'Milk, no Sugar' writings is that they weren't even supposed to be a campaign. Not the five columns in this book, or the three others that were published in the *Listener* but do not appear here – I did try to avoid boring readers – or the three or four columns that I wrote a few years ago for *Metro* magazine, or the 'essay' (that's what the editors called it) that appeared in a 1995 issue of something called *Planet*.

The truth is set out in the very first story I wrote on the subject. A freelance piece, it was published, appropriately, in the *Listener*, in the 28 November 1992 issue. Lamely headlined 'Depresso Coffee' (my suggestion, I seem to recall), it's a lively, chattering read, even more graceless than the way I write now – and right on the money. I was ahead of my time. I was prescient. I saw a smooth beast slouching towards New Zealand. I should have got a loan and opened an espresso slophouse.

The story blathers, 'A definite cafe society is now alive and flocking to the hissing chrome font installed in espresso bars, which have sprung up in alarming numbers over recent times. In the past month I have counted four new bars in Auckland; small town tearooms have noticed the trend and are shoving out on the pavement signs reading CAPPUCCINO HERE!'

Cappuccino, latte, espresso, double espresso, whateveresso.

Connoisseurs know what is what and will excitedly refer to these abominations as "damn good coffee", or "proper coffee", even "real coffee". A tip for the innocent: do not ask for black cappuccino, which my girlfriend did when she left the family farm to live in Wellington, and was humiliated by howls of laughter from the waitress.

' . . . Apart from their absurd refreshments, espresso bars also offer a scene. Major hang-out territory. This is another reason to avoid them like the plague, but painter John Reynolds actively disagrees. When asked the burning question, "How to save Auckland" (October *Metro*), he says, "We need more espresso bars. That would increase social intercourse and get the city's central nervous system ticking along." Reynolds is a familiar coffee-guzzling sight in Auckland and is rumoured to have a tab at his favourite espresso bar.

'No big deal, perhaps, except that espresso bars – progressive, vibrant, exclusive – spell a virtual end to tearooms. How quaint that word sounds already, as if it belongs to a misty past of trams, sixpences, free milk in schools. But when I think of two Wellington tearooms that sold out to espresso bar management, it's not with the sigh and glow of nostalgia; more like a sick disappointment at their loss.

'The Hob in Cuba Street and the Mandarin in Willis Street were both dark, faintly dingy places. Like their customers, they were cheap and quiet. I made countless visits for countless hours over 10 years. Mostly I went alone. That was the point: just to sit there and smoke, nibble on lamingtons and toasted sandwiches, sip beige-coloured coffee, stare out at the street, think about usually nothing very much, and wait for nothing at all.

'Both tearooms closed in 1989 . . . Similar places continue to close, mown down by the march of "real coffee". A few still exist and I track them down, continue my old habits. Friends laugh, dismiss this as an eccentricity, and head off for their social intercourse and their caffeine fix. When they travel overseas, the postcards are always the same: "Am in a groovy little cafe drinking GREAT cappuccino . . ."'

'New Zealand disappears behind them as they leave. Then they return with a very reasonable demand to enjoy the same consumer services as other countries; a market for espresso bars is built up, and a part of New Zealand disappears.

'I'm told it's no great loss. I tell them the jug has boiled, tap my jar of instant with a spoon, and ask them if they want milk or sugar.'

I married my girlfriend, Auckland has more espresso slophouses and I suppose more social intercourse for what it's worth, and I've been rewriting that story for nine years. The truth is just the same: the reason I write about tearooms and coffee lounges is because I am selfish. I'm happy that so many readers have written to me pointing out the whereabouts and virtues of tearooms all over New Zealand. And I do love Jenny's cover. But I never wanted to make a fetish or mount a campaign out of what is really a quiet affection. All I want is to mooch off to a tearoom, and smoke, and drink hot coffee poured straight from the pot and eat something I can pronounce, and stare out the window, and think nothing about campaigns, celebrations, columns – I just want somewhere to feel at home, content, unbothered, alone.

MANGROVIA

THERE IS A photo I like. It has the biggest mangrove tree in New Zealand in it – as photographed by Wade Doak, an underwater legend (his books are among the finest documented record we have of our marine life) and a man who knows his mangroves. Doak wrote to me a few months ago following this column's regular updates on the state of the mangrove creek that runs at the back of my Auckland flat. 'I share your passions,' he wrote. 'I have written, photoed, videoed, dived, crawled, built tree platforms, even lectured on mangroves.'

All of which makes me look like a dilettante in mangrovia. I pull on my gumboots and my protective gloves and waddle about cleaning up a creek which is really no more than a squirt of water. It takes about 30 minutes to walk its length. Only five or six steps are needed to cross its width. Doak is more concerned with the big picture: 'The risk of a major oil spill on the New Zealand coast has never been greater,' he wrote in the *Otago Daily Times* in July, warning that the likeliest danger zone is in Northland. 'I envisage a slick spreading up the Tutakaka coast from the impact point, devastating Ngunguru, Wananaki and Whangururu, and heading towards the Bay of Islands . . . I suspect New Zealand has virtually no resources to handle a supertanker disaster on our coast.'

And there I was going out of my mind with alarm and disgust in November because some idiots working on the nearby Woolworths supermarket were pouring paint down a stormwater drain and into my local creek. I left a phone message abusing the hell out of the contractors. Strangely, they never returned my call.

But I also got on the blower to a 24-hour environment hotline, and a bearded wallah turned up within a few minutes and sorted it out.

A month later, what was left of my mind once again filled with disgust and alarm because a mysterious spill of black-coloured water vomited into the creek. The authorities set up pumps and drained the creek right down to the mud floor. Not a pleasant sight. I got yarning to a few of the workers. One of them said, 'What this creek needs is to be completely dredged and then filled in with concrete.' It struck me that I had met perhaps the biggest fuckwit this side of Australia, but a few days later some trout from the *New Zealand Herald* came to my door looking to write something about the spill. By then, most of the black scum had been siphoned off.

'A pity there's no dead fish,' said the trout.

'Now why do you say that?'

'Cos it'd make a good story for the paper.'

The scum, as they say, also rises.

Rather more helpfully, several readers – Robert of Riverton, Joan of Christchurch, Matt from Planet FM in Nelson, Charlotte from up the road – have been in touch to say that they, too, go about cleaning their parks and beaches. I also got a letter from the Ron Greenwood Environmental Trust in Wellington inviting me to apply for 'some modest funding' in my efforts to keep the creek in good nick. What a nice gesture, and much appreciated, but I'm all right for gumboot and gloves expenses, thanks.

God also wanted to lend a hand, through his Anglican representative Reverend Jim White of All Saints Church in Ponsonby. White wrote offering 'general support and a couple of specific offers of help . . . We [the parish] would be glad to hear your reflections and suggestions.' I made an appointment to meet him at the church. Unfortunately, I turned up drunk off my ass, stank out his office with the smell of cheap liquor, and never heard from him again.

A shame. I liked the idea of some godliness being next to the creek's vile uncleanliness. 'Should I go on *Holmes* and threaten to drink the water on national TV (after sorting out my will)?' emailed Jay from up the road, speculating about ways to force the council into action. Yes, yes, the creek stinks and the creek reeks. But the problem with eco-whingers is that they hardly ever tell you about the loveliness of nature. As such, I regret missing Pauline Thompson's apparently really good exhibition of mangrove paintings at the Judith Anderson Gallery last year. Cheers to Pip who emailed to recommend Annie Dillard's book *Pilgrim at Tinker Creek*: 'Essentially it's all about spending time at a creek.' Will read. Thanks also for Sean's emailed offer to escort me around his local mangrove ('On a moonlit night, when the tide is full, the mangrove bay fills up and is like a speckled African lake'), and to Graham of the Part-Time Paddlers Club, who has invited me to be a guest on a kayak outing along mangrove-lined streams from Laingholm to Riverhead. Will do.

Probably my favourite letter on the subject came from Charlie. 'They are truly an amazing plant . . . I have always been intrigued by how they survive that terrible reflective light when the sun is going down.' His vivid six-page letter included his first memory of mangroves, 45 years ago, when he was a child in Pukekohe.

The furthest south that mangroves grow in the world is in Kawhia. Charlie lives in Rangiora.

20 January 2001

LIFE AND DEATH

IN THE END, if you're lucky, you get to live to a ripe old age, drooling onto your pyjama jacket at six o'clock in the evening at the Golden Showers retirement home, entertaining wild fears that the postman is going to ride up on his bike one day and kill you in your bed, trying to figure out what the television newsreader is telling you, dying for a drink, and moaning, 'What's the use?' Your looks, your mind, your health will have all shot through. There is so much despair and tender misery to look forward to. Good one. It will seem preposterous that you once enjoyed a simple, happy day on the road with a couple of friends, tagging along because you felt like it.

A day in summer. The sunshine pouring down, hot and thick and unstoppable. You are wearing a short-sleeved white shirt and a pair of pants you wore in December to milk the cows in a shed in Uruti. Your jandals cost $7 from Payless Plastics. Your feet have tan lines where the jandal strap arches out from your big toe.

There is the motorway, and the mangroves at high tide – James K. Baxter spent the last weekend of his life looking for a child's gumboot in an Auckland mangrove swamp. There is the cheese shop in Mercer, and the Waikato River lying on its back. Last night you read a book written by a 19th-century naturalist travelling up the Amazon River. He ate turtles and something called a cow-fish, and his pet toucan fell overboard and drowned, which inspired him to write that perfect, shimmering sentence, 'I missed my toucan.'

You are blathering on about knocking back seven Sigh of the Moor cocktails at the Alhambra on Friday night, and how you swam beneath the limb of a pohutukawa tree at a Herne Bay beach on Tuesday afternoon. You drive past Huntly and Ngaruawahia – why are there all these green metal pillars sticking out of an empty field beside the main street of Ngaruawahia? – and Hamilton and Te Awamatu.

And then you stop for a cup of tea and delicious toasted sandwiches made with three slices of bread at Stephie's Place in Kihikihi. Across the road, at Little Weka pet supplies, you buy some grass weed from a bucket for your goldfish. There is a woman and her young daughter behind the counter. The white stucco building used to be a doctor's surgery, but Kihikihi no longer has a GP. The girl says, 'I went to hospital once, eh, Mum.'

Just past Otorohonga, the air cools, and there is shade on the roads, and the trees have some colour in their cheeks. Water drips from bamboo sticks in the Japanese Gardens in Te Kuiti. The town smells of cow. At the Wheels truckstop cafe, a blue rig called Ridin' Low sneezes into the carpark. There is a long, low crypt made from red brick on top of the cemetery, and black smoke rising from a distant hill.

You buy a copy of *Peace at Last: The After-death Experiences of John Lennon* by some New Age nutbag in a clearance sale at the library for 20 cents. 'My first direct encounter with John came three nights after his death. He didn't say much on his first visit . . . During the time we spent together, John asked me many times, "Will they believe?"' There is an after-death interview conducted in January 1982. 'Q: Will you be relating musically to Earth again? A: Yes. I plan to introduce a couple of albums that relate to my experiences here.'

But the real miracle at the library is Willie, a three-year-old cat of monstrous size. 'He's on a special diet,' says the librarian, and it must be very special indeed. Willie is as big as a hog. But he is a top bloke, friendly and trusting, who was found in the bonnet of a car and now has his own XXOX catflap in the library.

You head back north at five o'clock, and recommend the driver take the Otorohonga-Ngaruawahia turn-off on State Highway 31, because this is one of the loveliest, strangest 67 kilometres of road in New Zealand. It feels forgotten. The roadside grass is long haired. There is so much yellowness in the fields, in the clay, in the light.

A handle of Waikato beer at Pirongia. The town is open for business in the three best ways – a pub, a tearoom, a butcher shop. Jovially, it also has a street directory. Outside in the garden bar, bits and pieces of traffic drive past. This is about as close as the North Island gets to being the South Island.

The lights are turned off at Golden Showers at eight o'clock. The edges of shadows on the ceiling are as sharp as knives. 'Nurse!' wails poor old Mr Wilson across the way. 'Nurse!' Your feet are cold even though you are still wearing your slippers. You have no idea what day it is, or how you got here, and you are remembering a late summer afternoon with a glass of beer in your hand and someone laughing and the colour of yellow.

10 February 2001